THE COLOR LINE

The Color Line provides a concise history of the role of race and ethnicity in the US, from the early colonial period to the present, to reveal the public policies and private actions that have enabled racial subordination and the actors who have fought against it.

Focusing on Native Americans, African Americans, Asian Americans, and Latino Americans, it explores how racial subordination developed in the region, how it has been resisted and opposed, and how it has been sustained through independence, the abolition of slavery, the civil rights movement, and subsequent reforms. The text also considers the position of European immigrants to the US, interrogates relevant moral issues, and identifies persistent problems of public policy, arguing that all four centuries of racial subordination are relevant to understanding contemporary America and some of its most urgent issues.

This book will be of interest to students and scholars of American history, the history of race and ethnicity, and other related courses in the humanities and social sciences.

David Lyons is Professor Emeritus at Boston University, Massachusetts, USA. He previously taught at Cornell University in New York from 1964 to 1995. Focusing on moral and political theory, his previous books range from *Forms and Limits of Utilitarianism* (1965) to *Confronting Injustice* (2013).

By the same author

Forms and Limits of Utilitarianism
In the Interest of the Governed
Ethics and the Rule of Law
Moral Aspects of Legal Theory
Rights, Welfare, and Mill's Moral Theory
Confronting Injustice

THE COLOR LINE

A Short Introduction

David Lyons

Routledge
Taylor & Francis Group

NEW YORK AND LONDON

First published 2020
by Routledge
52 Vanderbilt Avenue, New York, NY 10017

and by Routledge
2 Park Square, Milton Park, Abingdon, Oxon, OX14 4RN

Routledge is an imprint of the Taylor & Francis Group, an informa business

Library of Congress Cataloging-in-Publication Data
A catalog record for this title has been requested

ISBN: 978-0-367-85651-9 (hbk)
ISBN: 978-0-367-81892-0 (pbk)
ISBN: 978-1-003-01417-1 (ebk)

Typeset in Bembo
by Newgen Publishing UK

To the memory of Elmer Sprague (1924–2019) – teacher, mentor, and friend.

During all the years of their bondage, the slave master had a direct interest in discrediting the personality of those he held as property. Every man who had a thousand dollars so invested had a thousand reasons for painting the black man as fit only for slavery. Having made him the companion of horses and mules, he naturally sought to justify himself by assuming that the negro was not much better than a mule. The holders of twenty million dollars' worth of property in human chattels procured the means of influencing press, pulpit, and politician, and through these instrumentalities they belittled our virtues and magnified our vices, and have made us odious in the eyes of the world.

Frederick Douglass, "The Color Line," The North American Review,
vol. 132 (1881), p. 573

It would be only fair to the reader to say frankly in advance that the attitude of any person toward this story will be distinctly influenced by his theories of the Negro race. If he believes that the Negro in America and in general is an average and ordinary human being, who under given environment develops like other human beings, then he will read this story and judge it by the facts adduced. If, however, he regards the Negro as a distinctly inferior creation, who can never successfully take part in modern civilization and whose emancipation and enfranchisement were gestures against nature, then he will need something more than the sort of facts that I have set down. But this latter person, I am not trying to convince. I am simply pointing out these two points of view, so obvious to Americans, and then without further ado, I am assuming the truth of the first. In fine, I am going to tell this story as though Negroes were ordinary human beings, realizing that this attitude will from the first seriously curtail my audience.[1]

W.E. Burghardt Du Bois, Black Reconstruction in America:
An Essay Toward a History of the Part Which Black Folk Played in the Attempt
to Reconstruct Democracy in America, 1860–1880 [1934]. In The Oxford
W.E.B. Du Bois, vol. 6, p. xliii. Copyright 2007 © by Oxford University
Press. Reproduced with permission of the publisher.

---

1 For "Negro," today's reader should substitute *person of color*, and pronouns should be gender-neutralized.

CONTENTS

ACKNOWLEDGMENTS

I am grateful for research assistance to Jenna Fegreus, Stephanie Weigmann, David Aleksic, Matthew Bourque, Kate Cimini, Nam-Giao Do, Nir Eisikovits, Michael Fogleman, Eva Gach, Adam Goodstone, Buck Haddix, Nathan Hammonds, Michael Hinds, Travis Hubble, Charles Hunter, Lauren Ingoldsby, Chelsea Johnson, Peter Kawalek, Atif Khawaja, John Koss, Miriam Mack, Da Mao, Brendan McVey, Sindi Mncina, Ashkan Mojdehi, Kathleen O'Malley, Jonny Schreiber, Alyssa Slater, Matthew Smith, Tagore Subramaniam, and Beth Walker. I am grateful for comments and suggestions on earlier drafts to Emily Lyons, Jeremy Lyons, Matthew Lyons, Sandra Lyons, Louis Hutchins, and anonymous readers for Routledge. My thanks to Eric Scarffe for the Index, to Fintan Power for copy-editing, to Zoe Forbes for guiding me through the publication process, and to Kelly Winter for managing the project.

1
INTRODUCTION
The Color Line

Americans generally see themselves and are seen by fellow Americans as white, black, red, yellow, or brown. These assignments are not primarily descriptive. They place Americans within a set of racial categories, in which whiteness confers status and privilege. This color line, which is joined to the ideology and practice of white supremacy, is a founding pillar of American society.

When Europeans first came to America, they saw themselves as civilized Christians and as superior to the indigenous peoples they accosted, who they were prepared to subjugate and dispossess of their lands. As some Native Americans and enslaved Africans became Christians, however, religious affiliation could not continue as a reliable qualification for social privilege. Color, which Europeans also used to distinguish peoples, became a more useful tool of social division. Colonies like Virginia would restrict enslavement to non-whites, for example, and when the former colonies joined to become the United States of America, its Congress would soon declare that newcomers could become US citizens only if they were white.

The importance of the color line is suggested by the fact that, for most of American history, whiteness has been more valuable than citizenship. Someone who was classified as non-white could be (or could become) an American citizen, by treaty, birth, or legislation, but their citizenship did not carry equal rights. Residents of the northern half of Mexico, which the US annexed after the Mexican American War, became US citizens under the Treaty of Guadalupe Hidalgo (1848), for example, but these new Mexican American citizens were not regarded as white by the dominant American society and were subjected to systematic discrimination, segregation, lynching, and deportation. Following the Civil War (1861–65), the newly amended Constitution not only abolished slavery but also conferred US citizenship on anyone who was born in the US. But the legal subordination of African Americans was soon reestablished under the system called Jim Crow, which ensured that they could be systematically exploited, raped, and lynched with impunity. Although Puerto Ricans (in 1917) and Native Americans (in 1924) were made US citizens by federal legislation, they remained on the wrong side of the color line, still subject to systematic discrimination. During World War II, the US government interned more than a hundred thousand Japanese Americans in concentration camps, most of whom were US citizens. It did so without a trace of the due process that the Constitution guaranteed, although no federal agency had reason to believe that their imprisonment was required by "military necessity." In other words, the color line renders persons of color *second class* citizens.

Despite twentieth century civil rights reforms, the color line remains linked with significant inequities. Some of them reflect persisting discrimination, but others are the entrenched legacy of past discriminatory treatment. Public and private policies have prevented many black families from buying homes they could have afforded, for example, and thus from acquiring financial resources that could soften the impact of illness, accident, or unemployment. A massive percentage of black families remain confined to urban "ghettos," with inferior schools and services and greater exposure to environmental dangers as well as exacerbating stress.

The chapters that follow provide a brief introduction to the history of the color line in America – America's racial history. That story is offered in the belief that we can best understand how to overcome racial inequity by learning how we got here. Before we embark on that narrative, however, some further remarks about the color line are in order and some aspects of its relations with other important aspects of American development should be emphasized.

Only European Americans have been classified as white, but that privileged assignment is not automatically conferred. In the first place, any non-white ancestry conventionally disqualifies one for whiteness in America (which shows how one's assigned color is not descriptive). Secondly, some self-styled white Americans have questioned whether immigrants from Ireland as well as those from southern and eastern Europe (especially Catholics and Jews) are *truly* white. Over time, most European immigrants have been credited with whiteness, but recent developments confirm that America retains a deep well of ethnic bias that is capable of generating geysers of anti-Semitic violence and of finding new targets, such as Muslims.

A society's dominant ideology is not accepted by all of its members. Not only have Americans of color resisted discrimination; there have always been whites who opposed the color line, or at least some of its most egregious manifestations. Many whites condemned the horrific slave trade, and some condemned slavery itself. Some whites opposed not only lynching but the brutally oppressive system of Jim Crow. Some white Americans have devoted their lives to combatting racial inequity, and some have given their lives in that struggle.

But the color line is not easily erased. After slavery was abolished (1865), Congress sought to socially reconstruct the slave societies of the former Confederacy, partly by mandating equal protection of the law and voting rights, regardless of past enslavement. African Americans, including former slaves, then participated in civic affairs and helped to institute major reforms, such as the creation of public schools in the South. But the reforms of Reconstruction were intensely resisted, and the resistance included a great deal of lethal violence. Federal courts undermined the project, many in the North did not support it, and the federal government soon abandoned it – allowing the former slave states to design and consolidate Jim Crow. It then took another century, great sacrifice, and fortuitous circumstances for supporters of racial equity to get the US government finally to denounce white supremacy and take significant steps against it.

Once again, however, every reform has faced substantial resistance and back-lash. As a result, racial segregation in housing and schools has in some places (most notably in the North) intensified since the civil rights reforms of the 1950s and 1960s. Voting rights, made accessible by the enforcement of new federal legisla-tion, are once again being undermined by state laws, with the acquiescence of federal courts. And even the most ambitious reforms have failed to address deeply entrenched racial inequities, such as the wealth gap between white and black fam-ilies. So the life prospects of a child of color – her access to healthy surroundings, medical care, good schools, decent jobs, and economic security – remain markedly inferior to the life prospects of her white peers. The American promise of equal opportunity remains for many an elusive dream.

The narrative that follows focuses on five groups – European Americans, Native Americans, African Americans, Latino Americans, and Asian Americans. These wide categories are themselves products of color line thinking. Just as Europeans coming to America have initially thought of themselves as, say, English, Irish, or German, indigenous peoples have seen themselves as, say, Narragansett or Wampanoag – and so on, for the other communities of color. The wider categories, such as American Indian, which were initially used by whites, were adopted by those so labelled as they came to recognize that they shared important interests with other Americans of the same broad category.

The terms with which we refer to Americans of color, however, can obscure their differing historical relations to America. Well-meaning European Americans sometimes say, "We are all immigrants, or children of immigrants." But that ignores important aspects of American history. Native Americans did not immigrate; they were driven off their lands. Puerto Ricans and many Mexicans did not immi-grate; they became Americans when the US seized their homelands. Also, some immigrants of color have come voluntarily, but others arrived in chains. These historical differences ground differing claims for reform and possible reparations.

The color line does not define America, nor is it the only significant fault line of American society. Many whites face dismal life prospects, and inequality among whites is greater than ever. Women remain subject to sexual harassment, assault, and subordination, at home as well as in the workplace, as is also true of those who identify with non-traditional genders. These inequalities are greatly compounded when combined with residence on the disadvantaged side of the color line. That phenomenon of "intersectionality" multiplies the harms, deprivations, and stresses of subordination.

Thus, the color line is only part of the American story. But it is a central part, and it is the history we shall trace.

Now to note some other crucial aspects of that history, beginning with America's involvement with colonialism.

American Colonizing

The original and primary pattern of America's colonizing has been *settler colonialism*, which involves displacement of the indigenous population by outsiders. (By contrast, the British colonization of India involved no such displacement but rather rule by a small corps of outsiders who were aided by indigenous subordinates.) Once the first settlements were established, Europeans came to America by increasing numbers, many seeking the independence and security that landownership seemed to promise. Newcomers came to regard Native Americans as obstacles to settlement, who could justifiably be displaced by whatever means might be necessary – all the more so when the indigenous population resisted displacement.

European settlers initially lacked the power simply to drive away Native Americans, and European political units (first the several colonies, then the US government) dealt with them diplomatically. As the population balance shifted, however, the newcomers pushed settlements further and further west, always displacing the indigenous population, in most cases ignoring and thus cancelling treaty-based guarantees to Indian tribes of their territory.

American colonizing that is of significant relevance to the color line has also taken other forms. The US acquired territories by purchase (Louisiana, Alaska), by war (northern Mexico, Puerto Rico, the Philippines, and much land that was ceded by Native American nations), and by force-backed subversion (Hawai'i). Some of the acquired territories were divided into units that eventually became states of the Union (Louisiana, Oregon, northern Mexico), but not all: the Philippines was a colony (like British India) until it became independent, whereas Puerto Rico remains a colony today (with only so much autonomy as the US Congress decides it may have).

Those who authorized American acquisition of other nations, such as Hawai'i, the Philippines, and Puerto Rico, have justified their actions by claiming that the *brown* populations of the subordinated nations were incapable of governing themselves without the guiding hand of white-dominated America.

American relations with other nations of the Americas that remained nominally independent of the US have approximated colonization. After the Spanish–American War (1898), for example, Cuba became formally independent, but the US Army remained on the scene until the Cuban constitutional convention was persuaded to authorize America to intervene at will in Cuban affairs. The US military helped Panama secede from Colombia so that America could secure control of territory that would include a Panama Canal. The US military has intervened scores of times throughout Latin America, sometimes remaining as an occupying army for years, in order to secure American investments and gain control of state policies. American influence has often been maintained thereafter by helping selected members of the police or military secure high positions and employ dictatorial power.

After World War II, America's direct, overt military intervention (its "gunboat diplomacy") was limited to Grenada and Panama and was largely replaced by covert CIA regime-change operations for similar purposes (Guatemala, Brazil, Chile, El Salvador, Nicaragua, and Haiti – plus the failed invasion of Cuba). In that more recent period, it became politically imprudent in a global context for US government policies to be defended explicitly on color line grounds (as a matter of "helping our brown brothers" or the like).

Comparable American interventions outside the Americas – which have some-times led to interminable wars – lie outside the scope of the present work.

Slavery

Chattel slavery – slaves owned as private property – became a component of the English North American colonies, although the Common Law of England, which was inherited by those colonies, neither authorized the private ownership of slaves (which involves imprisonment, forced labor, and violent discipline) nor permitted other aspects of the institution that its colonies developed (such as sexual assault and slaves' children inheriting their parents' condition). Virginia did not bother to authorize chattel slavery until half a century after it began to import slaves; then it declared that slavery was limited to people of color – thus driving a social wedge between white and black working folk, who had previously joined forces against the colonial government. Thus, a racial caste system was institutionalized in America. As the vast majority of slaves in the colonies had African ancestry, the black–white dichotomy soon dominated color line thinking. Blacks were especially stigmatized, and a preference for lighter skin tones was internalized throughout American society. Millions of children and immigrants joined a society embodying a rigid color line, which before long seemed part of the natural order.

Slave-based agriculture became the most profitable branch of the American economy and the engine of its rapid development, North as well as South. Its products became America's most valuable exports by far, and slaves became the most valuable property in America (more on this below).

It is no wonder, then, that slavery was not seriously challenged during the Constitutional Convention of 1787. While compromises were required between larger and smaller states over representation in Congress and economic issues, the demands of states that were most dedicated to slavery, such as Georgia and South Carolina, were readily approved, without dispute. The result was a constitution that protected slavery directly (as by the Fugitive Slave Clause) and in various ways indirectly (too numerous to mention here) as well as by conferring disproportionate power (through the Three-Fifths Clause) on states whose economies and social systems centered on race-based slavery.

The profitability of slave-based agriculture as well as its depletion of the soil also created one of the principal pressures for territorial expansion. It led to the secession of Texas from Mexico (which had outlawed slavery) and America's subsequent war with its southern neighbor, which gave America the northern half of Mexico.

Racial Capitalism

It has often been assumed (not just by conventional Marxists) that capitalism requires a class of workers who are nominally free to sell their labor power to whomever they choose. On this view, societies whose economy centers upon unfree workers, such as the Old South, are "pre-capitalist," akin to feudal societies, ruled by a landed elite with a corresponding culture. Profits from slavery may then become "primitive accumulation" that is available for investment in emerging capitalist enterprises. This views the American economy as developing on two separate, independent tracks. That would misrepresent the relations between slavery and capitalism in America.

Slave-based agriculture was an integral part of the larger American economy, and arguably its driving component. The importation of slaves required and thus promoted shipbuilding, supplying the raw materials for that purpose, provisioning the ships, and supplying their crews, which were mainly Northern enterprises. The purchase of slaves often involved borrowing for the purpose, while insurance secured their value, thus promoting the development of America's finance, banking, and insurance industries. Owners of large plantations with many slaves were keenly aware of the returns on their investments, which led to a drive for efficiency, new modes of plantation design, and sophisticated accounting. The marketing of slave-based products required the construction of railroads, canals, and ships, which were also required to bring food and other supplies into regions that had become dedicated to very profitable slave-based monocultures. The cotton that slaves produced was processed in mills that were constructed for the purpose in the North, the looms and other machinery for which had to be manufactured, which spurred America's heavy industry. And so on. The antebellum American economy embodied what is now termed *racial capitalism*.

A note on terminology. In what follows, the terms used for places and social groups were chosen because they are familiar, easily pronounced, and not disparaging. With apologies to other peoples of the Western hemisphere, "America" refers to the United States and the English colonies from which it evolved, and "Americans" are its residents and citizens. (But "the Americas" refers to all of the Western hemisphere, as does "New World.") "Black person" and "African American" are used interchangeably, as are "white person" and "European American" as well as "Native American," "Indigenous American," and "American Indian." "Latino" refers to an American who is descended in part from the people of Spain or Portugal (the latter of whom, of course, are not "Hispanic"), and "Asian American" refers to one whose ancestors were people of Eastern, Southeastern, or Southern Asia.

2

PRE-CONTACT NORTH AMERICA AND EUROPEAN COLONIZATION

Long before their first contact with Europeans, Native Americans created agricultural economies that supported huge cities and wide-ranging trade between diverse nations with a total population of many millions (estimates range from ten million to ten times that number). South America was more densely populated than North America, but the latter was home to hundreds of indigenous nations with complex social systems, stable economies, and well-established, permanent communities. Like societies everywhere, those in America rose, flourished, and declined, as did the once-great Cahokia civilization of present-day Illinois.

Many Indian nations were joined together in confederations, such as the Iroquois (or Haudenosaunee) of what is now the Northeast US and the Powhatan of the Chesapeake region, where the first permanent English settlement was established. At the time of European contact, some regions were dominated by powerful indigenous nations, such as the Aztecs in central Mexico.

The Atlantic seaboard, where English colonization in North America began, was home to scores of indigenous nations in which land was held in common and women exercised significant political influence. These communities lacked police and courts but did not seem the worse off for that, as they typically sought to resolve internal disputes instead of punishing wrongdoers. By all accounts, that system was effective. But America was not a land of perpetual peace. Competition between indigenous nations for territory or dominance within a region sometimes led to warfare (though it was not the "total warfare" that attacked noncombatants and destroyed food supplies, which Europeans introduced).

Europeans who came to colonize in the Americas saw themselves as authorized to do so. Papal pronouncements of the fifteenth century acknowledged conquests by Portugal in Africa and by Spain in the Americas and affirmed their right to employ *any* means that proved necessary to maintain and expand territorial acquisitions and enjoy economic monopolies in their respective realms, while seeking to spread the Christian faith (a mission that was brutally implemented by the Spanish but a minor aspect of English colonization). In 1496 England's Henry VII conferred similar rights upon John Cabot and his sons, with the proviso that one fifth of their profits would go to the Crown. The first charter of Virginia had similar provisions, anticipating (in vain) the discovery of gold, silver, and copper, such as the Spanish had found in their colonial domains.

Native Americans did not endorse (nor were they asked to consider) the European "doctrine of discovery," which held that a Christian nation could rightly claim lands that had not previously been claimed by another Christian nation. (US courts would officially embrace that presumptuous principle when the occasion arose, in the nineteenth century. Imagine the American reaction to such a doctrine applied here on behalf of, say, Muslim nations!)

Europeans had engaged in comparable ventures in the Middle East, known as the Crusades, where they contended with non-Christians over access to sacred sites and promoted European commerce. They had every reason to expect similar resistance from indigenous Americans, who had different religious commitments, their own economic interests, and a desire for independence. It is no wonder that Spanish and Portuguese colonizers included soldiers as well as priests.

A Spanish party under Christopher Columbus reached the West Indies late in the fifteenth century, where they were initially welcomed. When the guests discovered that their hosts had gold, however, the newcomers turned upon them and forced the indigenous population to mine for precious metals. The conditions of enslavement and the punishments to which Indians were subjected had catastrophic effects when added to the diseases, such as smallpox, that were carried to the Americas by Europeans, to which indigenous Americans lacked immunity. It is estimated that the Taino population of the Caribbean, for example, was reduced from one million to one thousand within a few decades.

Some Spanish colonizers, such as Bartolomé de las Casas, were appalled by their countrymen's practices and condemned their brutal treatment of Native Americans. De las Casas thought it would be better to bring enslaved Africans to labor for the Spanish (though, witnessing the results, de las Casas later regretted making the recommendation). Early in the sixteenth century Europeans initiated the transatlantic slave trade. Ever-increasing numbers of African slaves were needed, not only to expand the colonizers' economy but also to replace the victims of exceedingly harsh laboring conditions.

By the middle of that century, Spanish colonizers had secured control of the Americas' principal population centers outside of Brazil, sometimes by killing thousands of Indians. By the end of the sixteenth century, Spain and Portugal had one hundred and fifty thousand colonists and thousands of African slaves in the Americas. Spain developed the world's largest empire and secured enormous wealth from precious metals that were extracted by slave labor.

English colonizers reached Newfoundland just a few years after Columbus landed in the West Indies. But England suspended its American ventures for several decades, as it became preoccupied with its break from the Roman Catholic Church, the resulting conflict within England between those who remained loyal to Rome and those who accepted the officially sanctioned Church of England, and its own colonizing of Ireland.

England had invaded its Irish neighbor in the twelfth century, but at the time secured for the most part only the region around Dublin. Its colonizing of Ireland expanded after England broke with the Roman Church, to which Ireland remained loyal. By force of arms, England gained control of the entire island by the seventeenth century. England enslaved thousands of Irish, for sale abroad, claimed most Irish land, and established a plantation system in which the surviving Irish became tenant farmers. Protestant England excluded Irish Catholics from the vote, public office, and university education. It banned Catholic schools and the Irish press, severely limited Irish ownership and leasing of land, and penalized marriages between Catholics and Protestants.

England's activities in Ireland thus foreshadowed its policies towards Native Americans and Africans. In fact, some of the English who colonized Ireland moved on to comparable work in America.

England resumed its colonizing ventures to the New World in the 1570s, at first unsuccessfully. In 1607, however, the English established a permanent colony in what became Jamestown, Virginia, and in 1620 another in present-day Plymouth, Massachusetts. (I'll leave out the "what became" and "present-day" hereafter.) A dozen more settlements soon followed, in New England and Maryland.

The English also seized some Caribbean islands, beginning with Bermuda in 1609. Like other European colonizers, the English eventually dedicated those islands to sugar cane, on large plantations worked by many slaves. The so-called "sugar islands" became highly profitable for European planters but extremely unhealthy for their slaves, who were worked to death. The laboring populations of those islands could be maintained only by a steady flow of captives from Africa.

Most Spanish and Portuguese colonial undertakings were government-funded projects. By contrast, English colonial ventures were financed by private investors but licensed by the Crown. Perhaps for that reason, English colonizing parties lacked military contingents and were initially too weak to overcome indigenous resistance to English domination – until warfare, disease, and continued immigration enabled the English to overwhelm what remained of the local Indians.

English royal charters conferred colonizing authority on the Virginia Company and the Plymouth Company, gave them economic monopolies within their respective realms, exempted them from English taxes, and stipulated what percentage of their profits belonged to the Crown. The Virginia Company's charter anticipated rich rewards from the region's precious metals, and the Jamestown party included only men and boys, for the Company had not planned on founding a heavily populated colonial settlement.

The Plymouth Company, by contrast, intended to create a home for certain religious dissidents who sought a haven for whole families. Its charter also included profit-sharing with the Crown but did not mention precious metals. The Plymouth colonists expected a bountiful harvest of fish from the sea. Their charter also notes, with satisfaction, that epidemics among the Indians had already made room for settlements (which indicates that they had gathered some accurate information about the area). Indians of the region had been infected as a result of prior contact with European fishermen.

Decimation of the indigenous peoples was not unwelcome to English colonizers, who showed little concern to convert Native Americans to Christianity, although their charters imposed that commitment. The dominant attitude of the English was that Indians must provide them with aid and then vacate the regions of expanding colonial settlement.

Thus, Massachusetts began as a settler colony; as we shall see, Virginia would soon follow.

England's colonizing slowed once again in the middle of the seventeenth century, when the country underwent civil wars, the overthrow of its monarchy, the development of non-monarchical rule, and expanded its control of Scotland as well as Ireland. After the monarchy was restored in 1660, England turned once again to America. The Carolina colony was established south of Virginia in 1663 and Georgia was created a few years later, further south. Midway between Virginia and Massachusetts, Pennsylvania – earlier settled by Dutch and Swedish immigrants – received an English charter in 1681.

Other European nations had established colonies near the English settlements. Spain colonized Florida (which the English colony of Georgia now abutted) as well as California, along the way establishing the northern boundary of New Spain (which would later become Mexico).

Dutch settlements, begun in 1624, were centered in the Hudson River valley, between New England and Pennsylvania. Holland was the leading slave trading nation for much of the seventeenth century, and its North American colonies had many more slaves than the colonies in New England. Anglo-Dutch wars led to the English acquiring those Dutch colonies in the 1670s, when England also assumed dominance of the slave trade.

French settlements in North America were initially limited to trading posts along the St. Lawrence River and the Great Lakes, beginning with Quebec in 1608. For many decades, the French did not seek to expand those settlements, as they bought furs from and developed friendly relations with neighboring Indians. When France later claimed the entire Mississippi Valley, it came into violent conflict with England.

Thus European nations in the Americas sought riches, commerce, and settlements. They competed amongst themselves for trade and alliances with Native American nations, and those competitions sometimes led to full-scale warfare. On their part, Indian nations and confederations likewise vied with one another for trade and alliances with the newcomers. European colonies formed alliances with some Indian nations in order to gain advantages over other nations, and Indians exploited differences among the European powers. That crucial aspect of Indian strategy was severely limited after 1763, at the conclusion of the French and Indian War, which ended North American colonization by the French. As we shall see, the war also undermined relations between England and thirteen of its mainland North American colonies.

Let's now look more closely at the colonizing of North America by England.

3

EARLY VIRGINIA

Early Virginia merits our special attention because of its development of race-based slavery. In 1607 the Virginia Company's colonizing party arrived at Chesapeake Bay, in the northeastern region of Virginia. The party was at first attacked by local Indians, perhaps because of their earlier unpleasant experiences with Europeans. But Native Americans near the party's ultimate settlement were friendly and helpful. Numbering only a hundred men and boys, the English newcomers presented little threat. The Chesapeake region was home to twenty thousand Native Americans; most of those near the new Jamestown settlement were united under Chief Powhatan.

The English had hoped to find gold and silver, which they would force Indians to mine, as the Spanish had done in their New World colonies. But the English were in no position to make the Indians do their bidding. Besides, the Virginia Company had guessed wrongly about Virginia's natural resources.

Ill-prepared for the hard work of establishing a new settlement, only sixty-eight of the party survived its first year, as many fell victim to disease and starvation. From 1607 to 1616 twenty-one hundred more settlers arrived, of whom only three hundred and fifty survived. Losses would have been much greater, had Chief Powhatan not sent them food.

The English traded iron implements, which Native Americans quickly came to value, for Indian food, land, and survival skills, all of which the newcomers urgently needed. But the colonists were not model guests. As their colony lacked a developed agricultural base and they quickly used up the supplies they had brought, they sometimes sought to obtain food from the Indians by force, and they seized land from which they expelled the indigenous residents. The Indians retaliated and, during Jamestown's first four decades, periods of English–Indian conflict alternated with intervals of coexistence.

Tobacco saved the colony. It was much desired in Europe, and colonists learned from the local Indians that it grew well in the Chesapeake region. The settlers began cultivating tobacco in 1612 and made their first shipment of it five years later. By then the colony had also become agriculturally self-sufficient. Those developments came too late to save the colony's parent company, however, which went bankrupt in 1624. The King revoked its charter and made Virginia a royal colony.

To generate increasing profits from tobacco, more land and workers were required. Land would be taken from Native Americans, which became easier to do as the population balance shifted in favor of the colonists. For immigration continued to enlarge the colony while the Indian communities were decimated by diseases that were carried by the newcomers. By 1640 the colony's population reached eight thousand and by 1670 forty thousand, while the Chesapeake's Indian population declined to less than three thousand.

As for labor, English colonial landholders relied on workers from abroad – first from Western Europe, then increasingly from West Africa. About half of those who joined the Virginia colony during its first century began under indentures, which legally bound one to work for a given period of up to seven years, in exchange for the passage from England and subsistence during the contractual term. At the end of that period, one was entitled to "freedom dues," such as tools, clothing, and a plot of land or a substantial quantity of tobacco.

Some English men, and before long women, took indentures in order to escape from unemployment or indebtedness, which were widespread in England at the time. The English enclosure movement, which had begun in the sixteenth century, transferred common lands to private owners and converted land from crops to pasture, which drove out tenant farmers. And the practice of primogeniture, which limited inheritance to the oldest son, contributed to widespread poverty in the countryside.

Others who became indentured had less choice in the matter: some were kidnapped, as a profit could be made by their captors when they were transferred to ships' masters, after which they would be auctioned off in Jamestown; and large numbers of Irish and Scots as well as some religious dissidents were forced to become indentured servants in England's colonies.

Some who came to America had been convicted of a crime in Great Britain, but instead of execution or imprisonment received the sentence of "transportation" to a colony, where they would serve under indentures. Only a few dozen convicts were sent to America before the middle of the seventeenth century, after which about ten thousand were transported there. The colonies were not usually happy to receive convicts, but they could not overcome the English government's determination to continue the practice. (When the colonies became independent of Great Britain, convicts would be sent to Australia instead.)

A small minority of English colonists had the wherewithal to pay for the passage of servants to America. Under Virginia's "head right" system, a colonist could claim fifty acres of land for each person he was credited with bringing to the colony. In this way, the wealthiest settlers increased their holdings in land, labor, and tobacco, and their influence expanded accordingly.

The year 1619 brought three important developments. The first contingent of women came, reflecting the colony's changed objectives: the Virginia Company recognized that their investment would be lost unless the colonists gave up seeking precious metals and sought profits from the land – an aim that by then seemed feasible, given the settlement's rapidly increasing tobacco exports. It was assumed that the importation of women would encourage the development of families and family-based agriculture to complement the production of tobacco. That same year, Virginia established a legislative assembly. Its House of Burgesses has been called a representative body, but the franchise was limited to land-owning males and the legislature was dominated by the largest landowners, who were referred to as the "Tidewater Aristocracy."

Also in 1619 twenty-plus Africans came off a Dutch ship when they were traded for provisions. As the Africans had been transported as slaves and were treated like property, this might seem to mark the introduction of slavery to England's North American mainland colonies. That is only half true. Surviving colonial records do not tell us the fate of those twenty-odd Africans. While some or all might have been subjected to enslavement, that could not have been done lawfully.

Unlike the law in Spain and Portugal, English law did not authorize slavery (it did not even regulate serfdom, which had long disappeared from England). As enslavement involved imprisonment (keeping a person against her will), forced labor (its main purpose), and assault (which was used to establish and maintain obedience), unauthorized enslavement was incompatible with the Common Law of England, which colonial charters prescribed initially for America. Slavery could be imposed as a punishment for crime, and laws authorizing the private ownership of slaves (and all that involved) would eventually be enacted in Virginia, but no such law was enacted until the 1660s. We'll return to that story below.

In 1622 deadly interactions between English colonists and Indians led to a major Indian uprising, which set Jamestown afire. Injuries and a food shortage that resulted from the attack cost the colony one third of its population. At what was to have been a peace conference the following year, the English served some Indian delegates poisoned wine and executed others. Warfare resumed and seizures of Indian land by colonists continued.

The indigenous uprising led the colonists to disregard their own culpability and to regard the Native American population as justifiably subject to attack and subjugation. As the colonists behaved accordingly, the Indians rose up again, in 1644; but the uprising failed once more to drive out the English. This time, however, the colonial rulers decided that their interests were best served by adopting policies that would discourage future uprisings. The two sides concluded a treaty in 1646, by which the Indians submitted to English rule and the colony accepted territorial limits. The treaty was respected by both sides for the next thirty years.

Among the Virginia colonists, the treaty favored the wealthiest landowners. Already possessing large and very profitable landholdings, they valued peaceful stability over expansion that risked more costly hostilities. But the arrangement eventually led poor white and black colonists to rebel together against the colonial government. Limits on land acquisition frustrated those who had served out their indentures and sought the economic independence that landownership could potentially secure. At the same time, Africans in Virginia were being adversely affected by colonial legislation that deprived them of many rights and that, beginning in the 1660s, institutionalized a racialized system of slavery (discussed in the next chapter).

In 1676 disputes by some colonists with members of a friendly, neighboring Indian community erupted into hostilities that became known as Bacon's Rebellion. Seeking to acquire land by killing or expelling Indians who resided beyond the colony's treaty-based boundaries, the disaffected colonists attacked members of other friendly Indian communities as well. As these actions violated the colony's official policy of peaceful coexistence with neighboring Indians, the colonial government intervened. In response, the rebels attacked the government, burning down Jamestown and forcing the governor to flee. The colonial government sought aid from England. By the time British troops arrived, however, the rebel leader, Nathaniel Bacon, had fallen ill and died, and the rebellion had ended.

But the local Indians had by then become sufficiently outnumbered to ensure their complete subordination. To escape further harassment by the colonists, some Native Americans sold their land and left the region to join indigenous nations further inland that remained independent. New treaties between the colony and its indigenous neighbors preserved some land for local Indian communities, but Native Americans who remained in the Chesapeake became menial workers.

It is worth pausing to reflect on the respective parties' attitudes. The records suggest that many colonists resented Indians' resistance to their demands, no matter how unreasonable those demands might be. The colonists wanted unrestricted acquisition of territory and food belonging to their indigenous neighbors. For several decades, the colonists could not simply seize either the land or the food supplies because they were too few and militarily too weak to dominate the indigenous population. Although the colonists were typically suspicious of the Indians' motivations, they favored coexistence when compromise seemed prudent. When they believed that they could act with impunity, however, they simply discounted the Native Americans' interests. Up to a point, these English attitudes resembled those they had towards competing Europeans, such as the French and the Spanish: they would take what others possessed if they could do so with impunity.

The Indians, although genuinely hospitable, may initially have accepted the newcomers because the English settled on undesirable land, were clearly too weak to represent a significant threat, and may have been seen as potential allies in the local Indians' own conflicts with competing indigenous nations.

When Bacon's Rebellion was over, the Tidewater Aristocracy faced a new set of problems. Black and white colonists had cooperated in challenging the colonial government and represented a threat to the colonial elite's power and security. What was to be done? The internal uprising appears to have hastened the development of slave law in Virginia, to which we now turn.

4

A SLAVE SYSTEM IS ESTABLISHED

As economic conditions in England improved during the seventeenth century, fewer English men or women sought alternatives abroad. Also, indentured service in the colonies may have become less attractive, to potential servants and masters alike. On the one hand, many servants died before they completed their indentures and, as land was not readily available, those who survived faced dim economic prospects instead of the desired independence. On the other hand, planters who wished to avoid the cost of freedom dues for those who completed their indentures, as well as the repercussions of former indentured servants' frustrations, recognized that slaves served for life and could be subjected to overwhelming discipline.

Although the English were active in the slave trade and relied upon slave labor in their Caribbean colonies, slavery was not a significant aspect of English society (more on this below), nor was it for several decades a significant aspect of England's mainland American colonies. Around the middle of the seventeenth century, however, the colonial government evidently decided to increase the colony's slave population, for in 1659 its legislature enacted the first Virginia statute to mention slavery, one that offered financial incentives to ships carrying slaves to Jamestown. Soon after, as a result of the Anglo-Dutch Wars, England took over not only the Dutch colony of New Netherland but also Dutch dominance of the trans-Atlantic slave trade. This enabled English colonists to purchase slaves more cheaply than before.

Once begun in earnest, Virginia's importation of enslaved Africans increased rapidly. The number of Africans in Virginia rose from three hundred in 1650, representing 2% of the colony's population, to sixteen thousand in 1700, 28% of its population, and more than one hundred thousand in 1750, fully 44% of Virginia's population.

For much of the seventeenth century, the legal and social status of Africans in Virginia was unsettled. Colonial records do not always distinguish between two classes of "servants" – those who were bound to serve for a limited period under indentures and those who were held in lifetime bondage. Records of court cases reveal, however, that some Africans served under indentures, and thus not as slaves for life, at least into the 1670s, while other Africans were subjected to lifetime servitude. Some African servants were able to purchase their own freedom and that of other family members, which means their masters allowed or enabled them to grow or manufacture things they could claim as their own to sell. Some Africans who had been servants acquired land and servants of their own. Racially mixed communities developed as well as communities of free African Americans (as they had by then become). Some African Americans were elected to public office, and there was inter-racial marriage – until the legislature intervened.

The colonial charters provided that the Common Law of England applied in the new settlements, but also authorized the colonial governments to make new laws, subject to Crown approval. The Common Law did not condone assault and prohibited holding another person prisoner against her will, and it drew no relevant distinctions between persons from Europe and Africa. It follows that slavery in the English colonies was unlawful unless an individual contracted freely into the condition, had been sentenced judicially to enslavement, had been captured in a just war, or was otherwise held with legislative authorization. None of those conditions was satisfied in 1619, when that first group of Africans was traded by the crew of a Dutch ship for provisions, or for a long time thereafter.

In thinking about the legal status of the Africans who joined the colony in 1619, we might be misled by the fact that they had been enslaved, were bartered for provisions, and thus were treated like property. Indentured servants were also treated like property, and yet they were not slaves, as they were held under contract for only a limited period, with rights to freedom dues upon the conclusion of their contracts. Prospective servants who disembarked at Jamestown without having prearranged indentures were subjected to a process that resembled a slave auction, as a result of which they were indentured to colonists who were prepared to pay the price, including a charge for their transportation to America. Once acquired as servants, however, those under indentures were treated by their masters much like slaves.

Not that the English were unfamiliar with slavery. They knew, of course, that Spain and Portugal had enslaved Native Americans and that they had been bringing Africans as slaves to the New World since early in the sixteenth century. By the seventeenth century, when the Virginia colony was established, many Africans were held as servants (or slaves) in England, having been brought there from abroad by English citizens or visitors. (The legal status of African servants in England was not clarified until 1772, when Lord Mansfield ruled, in the case of *Somerset v. Stewart*, that one cannot be enslaved in England except by explicit legal authorization.)

Nor were the English incapable of creating what amounts to slave law. Under the Vagrancy Act of 1547, for example, Parliament required unemployed workers to labor without wages for private parties. Those affected could be bought and sold, rented, given away, and inherited. Under the 1563 Statute of Artificers, workers between twelve and sixty years of age who lacked jobs, property, and apprenticeships were bound into farm labor for periods of years. The Scotland Act of 1606 made saltpan workers, coal miners, vagrants, and thieves bond slaves for life. They too could be sold, inherited, and the like. In the seventeenth century, tens of thousands of Irish were enslaved by the English and sold abroad as soldiers or as bond laborers for English colonies.

When the Tidewater Aristocracy perceived the economic benefits of slavery, the House of Burgesses enacted the necessary legislation. But they did so incrementally, as the need arose, long after enslavement had begun and after it was acknowledged in judicial proceedings.

The systems of slavery that Virginia and other European colonies in the Americas developed were different from the systems that already existed in Europe. In Spain, for example, slaves were prisoners of war or prisoners for debt who were bound into personal service for a limited period of time. Under Spanish law slaves could marry, marriage of slaves to free persons was allowed, and married couples could not be separated. Slave parents of ten or more children were freed. Manumissions were generally permitted and on holidays they were commonplace. Slaves had rights to good treatment that were enforceable in the regular courts. Excess punishment could lead to their freedom. Slavery was not inheritable, nor was it limited to certain social, ethnic, or religious groups. In all those respects, Spanish law differed from the law that was gradually created by English colonies in America.

Of course, the Spanish law of slavery was one thing, and Spanish colonial practice was another. Slaves in the Spanish and Portuguese colonies of the Americas were Native Americans or Africans, and thus were, unlike slaves in their respective home countries, ethnically distinguishable from their masters (with very few exceptions). And in the Caribbean sugar islands, European planters found it profitable to work slaves to death and then replace them. In most European New World colonies the death rate among slaves exceeded the birth rate, so a substantial slave trade was required just to maintain a working slave population.

(Slavery in the mainland English colonies was by no means benevolent, but by the end of the seventeenth century their slave population increased independently of the slave trade, perhaps because, unlike slaves on the sugar islands, for example, they did not work in the worst climates, on the largest plantations, or with the most physically demanding crops.)

Lifetime servitude is referred to in Virginia's court records as early as 1640, when a servant who had been captured after running away was sentenced to "serve his said master or his assigns for the time of his natural Life here or elsewhere." The sentence assumes that the servant was *not* already serving for life; he was presumably indentured.

The person so sentenced was identified as "a negro named *John Punch.*" His two fellow runaways, who were identified as Europeans, had their terms of service extended by only a few years. Punishing an African American more severely than European Americans for the very same dereliction is evidence of a developing color line.

An early official reference to pre-existing slavery occurs in 1655, when Elizabeth Key, identified as a "negro" who was being held as a slave, sued for her freedom and that of her child. The court found that Elizabeth Key's mother was a "negro" and a "slave," that her father was Thomas Key, a free man, and that Elizabeth Key had been christened. It was argued in court on her behalf that under English Common Law (1) a child inherits the condition of her father and (2) a Christian cannot be enslaved. In addition, (3) Ms. Key's master had acquired her with the understanding that her service was limited to a term of several years, which had long passed. A jury acted favorably on Ms. Key's petition. We do not know which of the arguments offered on her behalf was most persuasive but, as we shall see, we have reason to believe that the two Common Law arguments had repercussions beyond her case.

Also, we have no reason to suppose that Elizabeth Key's mother had contracted into slavery, had been taken prisoner in a just war, was sentenced to slavery as punishment for a crime, or that her enslavement had been authorized by colonial legislation. For (as we have noted) the earliest reference to slavery in Virginia legislation occurs later, in 1659, when the colony reduced its import duties on slaves in order to make Virginia an attractive place for slave traders to bring slaves for sale, which reflected Virginia's new policy of seeking slave labor. But that bare acknowledgment of slavery did not authorize or define the practice. Otherwise, the legislation that Virginia enacted in the years that followed would have been unnecessary.

Routine transactions such as contracts, bequests, and bankruptcies, as well as certain types of taxation, might have created the need to clarify the legal status of enslaved Africans. But events like Elizabeth Key's court case might also have done so. At any rate, the Virginia legislature began shortly thereafter, in the early 1660s, to construct a system of slave law, as the following enactments illustrate:

(1) In 1662 the legislature declared that "all children borne in this country shalbe held bond or free only according to the condition of the mother." This enactment may well have been motivated by a desire to forestall further uses of Elizabeth Key's argument that under English Common Law a child inherits the condition of her father. As the Crown did not object, it became Virginia law. Not only did the law make slavery officially inheritable, but it enabled slave owners to expand their slaveholdings by raping enslaved women – which was frequently done, with impunity.

(2) In 1667 the legislature declared "that the conferring of baptisme doth not alter the condition of the person as to his bondage or freedome." This enactment

may have been motivated by a desire to prevent further uses of Elizabeth Key's argument that a Christian cannot lawfully be enslaved. It was important because many of the Africans who came to early Virginia had been baptized in Africa or the West Indies or were baptized after coming to Virginia. As the Crown did not veto this enactment either, now Christians could lawfully be enslaved.

Virginia records include court cases involving servants who had been caught or otherwise returned after running away from their masters. These cases suggest that discipline and control were serious problems for those who held servants, both indentured and enslaved. As conditions for indentured servants in seventeenth century Virginia have been described as "nightmarish," we can understand why they ran away often enough to call forth remedial legislation. In 1642 the legislature prescribed penalties for persons found to have aided runaways; in 1657 it organized a militia to seek out runaways; and in 1672 it authorized the use of deadly force against runaways.

(3) The term of servitude could be extended as a punishment against an indentured servant who ran afoul of the law, but it could not be extended against one who was already being held for life. The legislature accordingly permitted more severe punishments for slaves who were already subject to lifetime servitude. One of its principal measures was an enactment of 1668, which declared that slave owners and their agents who kill slaves while disciplining them will not be guilty of a crime, because no one wishes to destroy his own property. The act assumed that punishments might be so severe as to endanger a slave's life, which is confirmed by the history of slavery. It gave masters the power of life or death over those they held in lifelong bondage and thereby added a provision that would become commonplace in American slave law.

The enactment may also have assumed that a slave owner was not likely to be found by a jury of his slave-owning peers to have maliciously killed his slave, because other slave owners could imagine themselves in comparable circumstances and would not wish to be held criminally liable for the death of their own slaves. The history of slavery also bears this out, for when masters were later made criminally liable for the malicious killing of a slave, there was little chance of their being held accountable.

(4) The enactment's language assumes that all slaves in Virginia were "negroes," although no law limited slavery to Africans. This may be understood as follows. Within a few years, the Virginia legislature would decide that people of color, and only people of color, including Indians, could be enslaved. But Native Americans who were enslaved in Virginia were generally sent abroad so that they could not readily escape from bondage. The law on the matter was clarified in 1682, when the legislature decided that "all servants ... brought or imported into this country ... whether Negroes, Moors, Mollattoes or Indians," whose ancestors were not Christian, "shall be adjudged, deemed and

taken to be slaves to all intents and purposes, any law, usage or custome to the contrary notwithstanding."

If the legal status of slavery was problematical before, its legality seems to be confirmed by this enactment. Given earlier legislation, which made slavery inheritable, no respecter of baptism, and compatible with life-endangering punishment, Virginia would seem by 1682 to have constructed a basic framework for slave law. No less important, this measure seems to announce officially, for the first time, that slavery was confined to people of color. The legislature had created a *race-based* labor system.

Why do that? One possible reason is that color-coding simplified enforcement, at least if the law presumed not only that all slaves were persons of color, but also that persons of color were slaves. That second presumption was encouraged by making Virginia increasingly inhospitable to free African Americans, most of whom then moved away. Another reason may be found in events that transpired shortly before the 1682 enactment – the events that comprised Bacon's Rebellion.

Conditions for indentured servants in seventeenth century Virginia were not much different from those for slaves. Servants from Europe and Africa lived and worked together and ran away together. This was facilitated by the fact that many of the Africans who first joined the Virginia colony were familiar with the English language and English customs as well as Christianity (some had in fact been baptized), as they came from the west coast of Africa, where by that time many Europeans were dwelling, and many had also spent some time in England's West Indian colonies. In 1676, as we have noted, poor black and white colonists joined together in Bacon's Rebellion. Colonists who had served out their indentures sought land. Given the legislature's recent endorsement of inheritable slavery and discrimination against free African Americans, black Virginians had additional grievances against the colonial government, which became a target of the rebels.

Bacon's Rebellion threatened a colonial elite more than any other uprising prior to the colonial rebellion a century later, which became the war for independence from Great Britain. The Tidewater Aristocracy's experience of confronting a united force of poor whites and blacks in 1676 may well have led them to conclude that their security would best be served by creating a race-based caste system. By consigning only people of color to the bottom, they accorded relative privilege, dignity, and opportunity to white persons, who might be expected to defend their superior position by helping to maintain African Americans' subordination. In 1682, only six years after the rebellion, the Virginia legislature decided that only people of color could be enslaved.

(5) To cement the color line securely in place so as to prevent inter-racial cooperation, the Virginia legislature discouraged fraternization between black

and white colonists. In 1691 it banned inter-racial marriages and punished inter-racial procreation (except, of course, when a white slave owner raped an enslaved woman). It sanctioned the killing of runaway slaves, provided that owners of such slaves be compensated at public expense, restricted the freeing of slaves, and required that freed slaves be transported out of the colony at the owner's expense. African Americans were to be excluded from normal relationships with European Americans.

(6) In 1705 the Virginia legislature constructed a slave code by collecting its prior enactments and elaborating upon them. It distinguished systematically between (white) indentured servants and (colored) slaves. In 1723 it enacted a second version of the slave code, which further restricted free African Americans as well as slaves and provided separate criminal proceedings for slaves.

Virginia thus created the legal structure for *a slave society*. The Virginia colony did not merely include slaves; its economy and social system was built upon slavery: slaves produced its principal products, and its lowest caste comprised only people of color, whether enslaved or (in decreasing numbers) nominally free.

Those new arrangements were effective. The doctrine of white supremacy was given material form and cemented white society together. As generations of white Virginians grew up in a system that consigned African Americans to the bottom, they were led to assume that racial subordination was normal. Within certain limits (stemming from the property value that slaves represented) white colonists could mistreat black colonists with impunity, while acts of self-defense by black colonists would be severely punished.

Virginia began as a community in which Africans and Europeans could develop cooperative, respectful, and intimate consensual relations, but it was forcefully transformed into a society that was built upon a brutally enforced racial caste system. Race-based slavery was not inherited by the colonists but was deliberately created by those who dominated the colonial government.

Virginia's slave-based economy and England's slave trade yielded riches for some in England as well as some colonists, so it is unsurprising that neither King nor Parliament interfered with the development of slavery in the colonies.

Many white as well as black colonists at the time, and later many white as well as black members of American society, disapproved of slavery and the color line. Angelina and Sarah Grimké, daughters of a South Carolina planter, argued in speeches and writings that the system not only violated the fundamental rights of those who were enslaved but had a corrupting effect on slaveholders and their families. Given the growing opposition to slavery, it is understandable that when the colonies achieved their independence from Great Britain, those who represented the centers of economic and political power in Georgia and South Carolina – states that were most committed to a slave-based economy – sought protection for slavery and the color line. Anti-slavery sentiment was not significantly represented in the Constitutional Convention of 1787, and delegates from both North and South readily agreed that a strengthened federal government should help to secure the system of slavery and the slave owners' most valuable property, their slaves. The delegates agreed that the defense of slavery and of property in slaves should be required even of those states that had abolished slavery or would soon do so (more on this below).

5

BEYOND VIRGINIA

We have paid special attention to early Virginia because of the significance of its gradual development of slavery. We turn now to note, in somewhat less detail, the creation and growth of other English colonies in mainland North America.

Following several failed ventures along the New England coast, the first permanent English settlement in that region was established in 1620 by religious dissenters called Puritans, who had earlier sought refuge in Holland. The Plymouth Company had secured a charter from the King for a colony north of Virginia, and a colonizing party of about one hundred reached Cape Cod, where they were attacked by local Indians, some of whose number had a few years earlier been kidnapped and enslaved by English visitors. The Puritans accordingly chose to settle off the Cape, at the abandoned Wampanoag village of Patuxet (now Plymouth).

Prior to contact with Europeans, the population of the region is estimated to have numbered more than a hundred thousand, three quarters of whom died from diseases that had been transmitted by Europeans. In Patuxet the newcomers found graves and unburied skeletons, evidence of such a scourge. The newcomers helped themselves to valuables and food that they found buried there.

The settlers were accepted by the local Wampanoags, who had been severely weakened by the epidemic and may have seen the English as possible allies in their rivalry with the nearby Narragansetts. Over the first winter, however, illness reduced the colonizing party by half. But the colony survived, partly due to aid they received from their Native American hosts (as happened in Virginia).

As immigration continued, English groups (not all of their members Puritans) established settlements further north, such as Salem and Boston, as well as along the more southerly coast. The newer settlements were also accepted by local Indians, who were in any case too weakened by the epidemics to put up much resistance. English ships brought twelve thousand new colonizers in the 1630s alone.

Thus one big initial difference from Virginia is that the Massachusetts settlements were located where Indians had already been decimated by disease. Other differences involved their aims and developing economies. Virginia was initially planned as an outpost where precious metals could be readily obtained, but became dedicated to the cultivation of a profitable cash crop, whereas Massachusetts was sought by its organizers as a safe harbor, was not suitable for cash crop cultivation, and developed a diversified economy based on small-scale agriculture, fishing, lumbering, and shipbuilding.

Although those activities did not generate a demand for labor comparable to that of the Southern colonies, Massachusetts colonists acquired African and Indian slaves, who eventually comprised 8% of Boston's population and 2% of the colony's as a whole.

In fact, Massachusetts sanctioned slavery and the slave trade earlier than Virginia. In 1641 the colony produced a code of laws entitled *The Body of Liberties.* While provision number 10 made "man-stealing" a capital crime, provision 91 declared: "There shall never be any bond slaverie, villinage or Captivitie amongst us," to which it added "unless it be lawfull Captives taken in just warres, and such strangers as willingly selle themselves *or are sold to us*" (emphasis added; the provision also allowed slavery as a legal punishment). Taken together, provisions 10 and 91 meant that colonists were barred from forcing persons into slavery but could lawfully purchase, as slaves, persons who had been unlawfully seized and enslaved – which at the time comprised nearly all, if not all, of those who were available for purchase as slaves.

Moreover, after 1698, when England ended a royal monopoly on slave trading, the New England colonies became major participants in the trade – building ships designed for the purpose, providing the ships with provisions, and using the ships to transport slaves, all in conformity with *The Body of Liberties.*

In Massachusetts as in Virginia some colonists opposed slavery. Several spoke out publicly against the institution, including John Eliot in 1675 and Samuel Sewall in 1700. Boston's selectmen urged an end to the importation of African slaves in 1701. Anti-slavery sentiment increased as the eighteenth century progressed. At the same time, many colonists came to fear slave uprisings and other forms of slave resistance, such as arson, and the colony enacted laws that were increasingly restrictive of slaves.

Relations between colonists and Native Americans were central to Massachusetts life and policy. Given the colony's determination to expand, this was inevitable. In 1633 the general court invoked a supposed English right to take uncultivated land, which would have included land on which Indians engaged in hunting, an essential aspect of their economy. (If that doctrine had been applied in England, it would have authorized the taking of many uncultivated "parks" that were kept by the English elite.) Land was also acquired from Indians by purchase, by harassing Indians (e.g., by letting livestock graze on their fields) until they left, and by imposing fines for the failure to follow the colony's rules (rules the Indians had no part in making), which they could settle only by ceding land.

Dissension within the colony stemmed in part from such policies, which Roger Williams condemned as violating Native Americans' rights. After his resulting banishment in 1635, Williams and others traveled to what became Rhode Island, where they established a new colony on land that was offered by the Narragansetts. Soon after, they were joined by a group led by Anne Hutchinson, who had been excommunicated and banished from the Massachusetts Bay Colony for her rejection of Puritan doctrine. The Puritans did not welcome dissent.

The Pequots of Connecticut were one of the strongest, most independent Indian nations of New England. In 1637 the Massachusetts colony, seeking regional supremacy, enlisted the Narragansetts to join an attack on the Pequots. In a decisive encounter, colonists surrounded and burned a Pequot village in Mystic, Connecticut, killing most of its five or six hundred occupants – women, children, and elderly adults – and enslaving the survivors. The colonists celebrated the massacre, but the Narragansetts were appalled by the colonists' murder of non-combatants.

In 1643 the colonies of Connecticut, Plymouth, and Massachusetts Bay formed the New England Confederation. Joining strategically with the Mahoganies, the Confederation in 1645 persuaded the Massachusetts colony's former allies, the Narragansetts, to accept English rule and to cede substantial territory. Having witnessed the English massacre of Pequots, the Narragansetts acceded to the colonists' demands.

Given the rapidly increasing colonial population in New England – twenty-five thousand by 1650, sixty thousand by 1675 – and a diminishing population of Native Americans, the Confederation soon secured control of southern New England. But its dominance did not go unchallenged.

In 1675 desperate Wampanoags rose up against the colonists, laying waste frontier settlements in Metacom's (or King Philip's) War. Other Indian nations joined the uprising, but inter-tribal competition prevented the formation of a Native American united front. Casualties were heavy on both sides. The rebellion weakened within a year, Indian leaders were executed, and hundreds of Native Americans were enslaved.

Thus, by the last quarter of the seventeenth century, in Virginia and New England – the two initial regions of English colonization on the mainland of North America – indigenous nations of the Eastern Seaboard had been conquered. Other coastal conquests would follow; settler colonization was well underway.

In 1660 (following the English Civil War, the Commonwealth, and the Protectorate) the English monarchy was restored. Charles II rewarded some of his supporters with a charter for Carolina, a new colony south of Virginia. Slave-owning planters from Virginia and Barbados (which adopted a race-based slave code in 1661) led in its settlement.

When the Carolina colony was established, its territory was heavily populated by Native Americans, including the Creeks and other large and powerful Indian nations. Here, as elsewhere, Native Americans welcomed trade with

Europeans – and then became dependent on it. Deer skins were exchanged for guns, cloth, and other manufactured items. This led Indians to hunt for purposes of trade instead of their own use and shifted the focus of tribal economies from agriculture to hunting.

By the 1670s, however, Native Americans themselves became the principal commodity that was supplied to the Carolina colony, which was developing a race-based slave society. What emerged was a trading pattern like that on the west coast of Africa: European settlements were located in the coastal region, and members of indigenous groups who resided nearby went inland to seize and enslave members of other indigenous societies, who they sold or traded to European Americans in the coastal settlements. Tens of thousands of Native Americans were enslaved and sent to labor in Carolina or other English colonies.

Slaves comprised a larger portion of Carolina's population than that of any other English North American colony. By 1708 the Carolina settlements included fifty-three hundred white colonists, twenty-nine hundred black slaves, and four-teen hundred enslaved Indians.

Settler policies towards Native Americans provoked a desperate uprising in this region too. In 1710 the Tuscaroras rose up and killed scores of colonists. Although they received support from some other Indian communities, Carolinian slave traders recruited a fighting force from competing communities, such as the Yamasee, and in 1713 the Tuscaroras were defeated. Hundreds of Tuscaroras were killed and hundreds more were enslaved.

Two years later, the Yamasee, moved by similar grievances, led the most threatening Indian uprising of the colonial period, involving more than a dozen Indian nations. Because of continuing competition among Indian nations for European trade, however, inter-tribal unity continued to elude the resisters. The Yamasee and their allies were defeated, and many survivors were enslaved. Within a few decades of the first European settlement, Native Americans in Carolina had lost 60% of their number from enslavement, warfare, and disease.

The principal exception to the dominant pattern of Indian–European interactions was found in early Pennsylvania. In 1681 William Penn received a charter for a Quaker colony. Although disease had weakened the local Lenni Lenape Indians, Penn allowed settlement only on land that had been purchased fairly from Native Americans. As a result, peaceful coexistence prevailed there for thirty years.

When Quaker influence declined in Pennsylvania, however, relations between settlers and Indians deteriorated. Newcomers were not committed to fair dealing and coexistence with Native Americans. They sought cheap land, and land speculators sought quick profits. Familiar patterns of encroachment replaced respectful relations, inter-tribal competition was exploited, and settlers acquired land by fraudulent means. By the 1740s the Lenni Lenape (now called the Delaware) had been driven away, cheated by newcomers and humiliated by their former allies, the Iroquois.

Several factors thus enabled the English to achieve unqualified control of Massachusetts, Virginia, and other coastal regions within a few decades of English settlement. The indigenous population decreased precipitously, partly because of infectious diseases that immigrated with the Europeans. Indian nations competed for trade with the Europeans and sought European allies for protection and leverage against their own Indian enemies. Native Americans failed to offer unified, timely resistance against the newcomers' encroachments. The English exploited inter-tribal conflicts by forging temporary alliances with some Indian nations in order to conquer others. The prospect of profits in the New World and the pressures of poverty and persecution in the Old World brought Europeans in numbers that soon exceeded those of the surviving Indians.

English colonizers also confronted the French, whose aspirations expanded beyond trade to territory, as they sought to extend their control from Canada through the Mississippi River basin to the French settlement of New Orleans. Wars between France and England, beginning in 1689, were waged partly in North America, including the French and Indian War of 1754–63. When the English defeated the French, they became the dominant colonizing power in North America. France retained its Caribbean sugar islands but lost the Indian fur trade and its territorial claims east of the Mississippi River as well as to Canada.

The French departure adversely affected North American Indians, who could no longer play one European power against another. During the French and Indian War, most Indian nations in the region had allied with the French, whose traders in North America had previously been less expansionist than English settlers. Native Americans now confronted an increasingly powerful British presence (British rather than English, as the 1707 Act of Union had joined Scotland with England).

When the colonists, soon after, rebelled against Great Britain, most Indian nations would ally with the British against the colonists. This requires some explanation. Although Britain defeated France, it was not prepared to expand its own colonizing in North America. Wars on two continents had generated a substantial debt and an unwillingness or inability on the part of the British to maintain a massive military presence to contend with Indian resistance to colonial expansion. Britain imposed taxes on the colonists to help defray its debt, some of which had been incurred to protect colonial settlements during the French and Indian War.

In North America, Britain now faced a problem like that of Virginia's government a century earlier, which had led to Bacon's Rebellion. The colonial population continued to grow (it would reach nearly four million by the time of the first American census in 1790). Colonists seeking land saw territory that Europeans had not yet appropriated within the domains of powerful Indian nations west of the Appalachian Mountains. Additional pressure for territorial expansion came from land speculators (including some of the men who would soon become leaders of the War for Independence).

To minimize conflict with Indians of the interior, in 1763 the King issued a Royal Proclamation that prohibited the colonists from moving into territory beyond the ridge of the Appalachian Mountains. This made all land between the Appalachians and the Mississippi River into an Indian reserve and implied that its Native American residents would enjoy royal protection.

The Native Americans of that region viewed the situation differently. It was their land. No Indian nation had participated in the negotiations that led to the 1763 treaty that supposedly conveyed French territory to Great Britain. No Indian nation had ceded such territory to either France or Britain, and no Indian nation of the interior had been conquered by any European power.

It would have been difficult and expensive for Great Britain to enforce the Royal Proclamation, and Britain did not attempt to do so. Colonists ignored the ban on settlement beyond the Appalachians and poured into Indian country with impunity. Like the new taxes imposed on the colonists by Great Britain, however, the ban on western settlement helped to alienate the colonists from the Crown – just as, a century earlier, a comparable ban had set the Virginia poor against the colonial elite. Within a dozen years, the colonists' opposition to British imperial policies would result in a new colonial rebellion.

6

THE FOUNDING

Americans are taught to view the War for Independence as a conflict between aggrieved colonists and an oppressive British Empire that led to the founding of an independent nation with a representative government. In this section our concern is with the origins of the conflict and the impact of the Founding upon Americans of color, so we shall focus on the critical involvement of Native Americans and African Americans.

Many colonists, including some of the most prominent colonial leaders, favored unrestricted expansion beyond the Appalachian Mountains, into what Great Britain had wanted the colonists to regard as an Indian reserve. It is not that Britain favored Indians over colonists. It wished rather to minimize conflict with formidable Indian nations of the interior, because the recent war against the French and their Indian allies, which ended in 1763, had cost Great Britain dearly in both personnel and treasure.

The differences between colonial and Crown policies were recognized by Indian nations, who saw that many colonists sought their land as well as independence from Great Britain. As a consequence, the vast majority of affected Indian nations sided with the British against the colonial rebels. During the colonial rebellion many Indians fought with the British, which led many colonists to regard Native Americans as treacherous enemies. Indian towns and villages became a target for rebellious colonists and Indians suffered accordingly, regardless of their actual policies.

At the war's end, Native Americans were excluded from the negotiations that led to the 1783 Treaty of Paris which officially ended hostilities between the colonists and Great Britain. The Indian nations that had allied with the British were abandoned by them.

The treaty purported to transfer to their former colonies territory that Britain claimed between the Appalachians and the Mississippi River. As we have noted, the Indians who resided there saw matters differently. They were not parties to the treaty, they had not agreed to its provisions, and they had not ceded any of the lands to France, Great Britain, or the United States.

The new American government wished to avoid war with the Indian nations, as had Britain in 1763 and Virginia in 1645. So, in 1787 the Continental Congress adopted the Northwest Ordinance, which concerned the territory that lies northwest of the Ohio River, now claimed by the US. After the federal Constitution was ratified, the Ordinance was reaffirmed in 1789 by the new US Congress.

Article 3 of the Ordinance says:

> The utmost good faith shall always be observed towards the Indians; their lands and property shall never be taken from them without their consent; and, in their property, rights, and liberty, they shall never be invaded or disturbed, unless in just and lawful wars authorized by Congress; but laws founded in justice and humanity, shall from time to time be made for preventing wrongs being done to them, and for preserving peace and friendship with them.

As Indians of the region knew, however, this declaration was already being violated and in all likelihood would continue to be violated with impunity, as had happened in the case of the Royal Proclamation of 1763.

So a number of Indian nations joined together in a Western Confederacy to resist American appropriation of their lands. Their combined resistance was initially effective, as it led to military victories over US forces in the early 1790s. But in 1794 a newly organized US Army under General Anthony Wayne defeated the Western Confederacy decisively in the Battle of Fallen Timbers. A year later, in the Treaty of Greenville, nations of the Western Confederacy ceded a substantial part of the contested territory to the United States, in exchange for annuities.

It then became the federal government's turn to seek more stable and peaceful relations with Native Americans. In fact, Congress had already begun to take action. Beginning in 1790, its Trade and Intercourse Acts committed the federal government to protective oversight of land transfers from Indian communities to non-Indians and of commercial relations between Indians and outsiders. Unfortunately, while the federal government took some measures to regulate trade, it neglected its commitment to oversee land transfers, as US courts later confirmed. In 1975, for example, the Passamaquoddy and Penobscot nations were held to have retained valid claims to two thirds of the state of Maine because the federal government had not discharged the oversight responsibilities to which it was committed. Many other Indian land claims were soon validated by US courts. (Most such claims have since been settled, with Indian communities recovering modest parcels of land, but even now some claims in New York state remain contested.)

The federal government's failure to enforce the Trade and Intercourse Acts was not an isolated occurrence. A recurring aspect of American history has been white settler expansion at the expense of Native Americans, in violation of American laws, treaties, or public policy, which the federal government was unable or unwilling to enforce, as well as direct federal violation of treaties with Indian nations.

Let us now go back a few years to the colonial rebellion, which critically affected African Americans too. Both the rebels and the British were ambivalent about the recruitment of African Americans. Each side desired the additional manpower but feared that arming blacks would facilitate slave rebellions. African Americans did not wait for the combatants to make up their minds. In the North, despite discrimination by white colonists against them, many free black colonists joined the rebels. They took seriously, or perhaps hopefully, the rebels' explicit appeal in the Declaration of Independence to universal human rights, though it clashed with the color line – that is, with the practice and underlying doctrine of white supremacy. In the South, the war for independence diverted manpower from slave patrols and plantation management, enabling many slaves, perhaps a hundred thousand, to escape from bondage. Instead of appealing for their freedom, many slaves seized it.

One of the Crown's principal agents made a fateful decision early on. In 1775 Lord Dunmore, royal governor of Virginia, issued a proclamation promising freedom to slaves who joined the British Army. Some of those who escaped from bondage accepted the invitation and formed the governor's Ethiopian Regiment. Dunmore's action was so bitterly resented by slave-owning colonists that it converted many of them from loyalists to rebels. The Americans' military commander, George Washington (who held many slaves), had opposed taking African Americans into the Continental Army, but Dunmore's action helped Washington change his mind.

After the war, the British enabled some of their black recruits to retain their freedom by helping them leave the former colonies, but the British also left many behind. The former colonists did not hesitate to reaffirm white supremacy when they founded their new republic. Let us consider some of the official measures that were taken to reinforce the color line.

In 1787 delegates from the several newly independent states met in Philadelphia to revise the Articles of Confederation that loosely tied the states together. Their meeting would become known as the Constitutional Convention because it proposed an entirely new Constitution.

Slavery figured centrally in the delegates' deliberations, but not primarily as an issue to be addressed – not even by delegates from states that had already taken steps towards ending slavery (all of the New England states plus Pennsylvania and New York) or that would soon do so (New Jersey). Chattel slavery was vigorously embraced by delegates from the Lower South, especially Georgia and South Carolina, whose demands for its protection were met without significant resistance. Although slave-based industry was not a central feature of the Northern states' economies, it was important indirectly, as Northern firms supplied, insured, and supported slave-based agriculture in a variety of ways (more on this below).

In the Constitutional Convention, slavery affected representation in Congress, which concerned the balance of power between North and South and specific issues that divided the two regions. Each sector sought to maximize its influence in the new federal government. The North wanted import duties to protect its industry, while the South wanted freedom from duties so as to minimize the cost of its supplies. Delegates from states with many slaves proposed that representation in Congress be based on total population, including slaves. Delegates from states with few slaves argued that if representation was to reflect property in slaves, then it should count property more generally, which would tend to even the balance. The compromise reached was to include three fifths of the slave population for purposes of representation in the House of Representatives and to create a second legislative chamber, the Senate, in which all states would be equally represented.

The "Three-Fifths Clause" ensured the political power of the slave states in all three branches of the new federal government: it enhanced their representation in Congress and therefore in the Electoral College, which elected the President, which in turn affected appointments to the federal judiciary and other high governmental positions. It is understandable, then, that the federal government maintained policies that were favorable to slavery until the Civil War.

Convention delegates from the Lower South also insisted that the new government be pledged to protect their most valued institution – slavery – and their most valuable property – slaves. Without difficulty, they secured endorsement of a clause requiring all states to cooperate in the return of escaped slaves, a provision guaranteeing federal aid against slave insurrections, and an article protecting the international slave trade for at least twenty more years.

Although Northern delegates did not make slavery an issue in the convention, the demands of the Lower South for the protection of slavery did not signify paranoia. They reflected an appreciation of developing anti-slavery sentiment within American society. Quakers and Mennonites had been agitating against slavery for a hundred years. Influential anti-slavery literature was distributed widely by the Pennsylvania Society for Promoting the Abolition of Slavery. Northern states were abolishing slavery (though some very gradually) and the Northwest Ordinance (which was adopted by the Continental Congress at the time the Constitutional Convention was meeting) banned slavery in that substantial territory.

Anti-slavery sentiment was significant in the South too – at least the Upper South. Some slave owners, including Washington and Jefferson, acknowledged that slavery was morally indefensible. Some leaders of the colonial rebellion may have been influenced by their French allies, who mocked the colonial slave owners' claims of "enslavement" by the British government. Also, as economic conditions had changed, Virginia planters had a surplus of slaves who could be sold to buyers in the Lower South (which helps to explain the willingness of the slave states to accept an eventual end to the international slave trade). During the last decades of the eighteenth century, however, a number of slave owners in the Upper South chose to free slaves instead of selling them, the manumission documents revealing moral reasons for their economic sacrifice.

The proposed new federal Constitution was ratified by the several states by 1789, and the new federal government got to work, with a continued commitment to the color line. In 1790, for example, Congress decided that newcomers could become citizens only if they were free and "white." Two years later Congress banned African Americans from military service. And in 1793 Congress passed the Fugitive Slave Act, implementing the constitutional requirement that all of the states cooperate in returning escaped slaves to their legal owners. Other restrictions on free African Americans followed.

The groundwork was thus laid for the great expansion over the next seventy years of an economy whose engine was an enormously profitable slave-based agriculture.

7

KING COTTON

By the late eighteenth century, the virtues of cotton fabric, especially for clothing, were widely recognized. Raw cotton supply could hardly keep up with the demand or with the capacity of water- and steam-driven spinners and looms in Great Britain and New England. Long staple cotton grew well in the coastal areas of the Lower South but not so well inland where short staple cotton could thrive. But short staple cotton required separation of the fiber from the seeds, which was a slow, labor-intensive process. Development of the modern cotton gin in the 1790s solved that problem. The labor saved could now be devoted to cultivation of short staple cotton.

As had happened two centuries earlier with tobacco, the profits to be made by meeting the increasing demand for cotton led Southerners with the wherewithal to seek more land and labor. Suitable land lay west of Georgia and the Carolinas, in territory that had been acquired under the 1783 treaty with Great Britain. Slaves would provide the labor.

The vast majority of slaves in America had earlier been employed in the production of exportable cash crops such as tobacco, indigo, and rice. Hereafter cotton would dominate the Southern economy. And so would slavery.

At the time of the Founding, some had imagined that slavery would slowly disappear. (That notion was not entertained in the Lower South.) Instead, it expanded greatly, even after 1808, when Congress outlawed America's participation in the overseas slave trade. (As the federal government was unable to police the seas thoroughly, even with Great Britain's cooperation, the African slave trade continued despite the ban, although on a smaller scale than before.)

As the Upper South had more slaves than its economy required, it provided the basis for a very profitable domestic slave trade that moved African Americans from the Upper South (Virginia, Maryland, and Delaware) and the Atlantic seaboard to the newly acquired cotton-growing lands to the south and west. Congress's action against the international slave trade only increased the importance and magnitude of the domestic trade.

Cotton quickly became "king" – not only America's principal export of the antebellum period, but more valuable than all other American exports combined. Cotton production became the engine that drove America's rapidly expanding economy, which included Northern industries that serviced the plantations, from finance and insurance to food supply, as well as those that spun the cotton and wove it into cloth, those that manufactured and serviced the spinning machines and looms, and those that transported both raw and processed cotton. Thus, during the antebellum period, America's wealth, North and South, was built primarily upon slave labor.

Once again, the drive for land was disastrous for Native Americans. Shortly after the cotton gin was invented, the United States purchased the Louisiana territory (1803). This addition provided land west of the Mississippi River, to which Eastern Indian nations could be consigned, making more land available for cotton cultivation. That transformation required Indian Removal, which Andrew Jackson endorsed and as President would implement.

European Americans wished to take over all of the remaining land, North and South, that was reserved for Eastern Indian nations by treaty and other federal law. On the basis of boundaries that had originally been laid down in colonial charters, many states that began as colonies claimed territory that extended far west of the Appalachians. Given the ways colonial charters were written, many of those western claims conflicted. In the early years of the republic, most of the states had transferred those land claims to the federal government. In the North, this made possible the distribution of land to Revolutionary War veterans and the organization of territories to be developed into new states in the Old Northwest (the first being Ohio in 1803). Similar land transfers occurred in the South, which led to the formation of Kentucky (1792) and Tennessee (1796). Georgia was the last state to cede its western claims, in 1802, which made possible the establishment of Mississippi (1817) and Alabama (1819). Georgia had done so on condition that the federal government would convince the Cherokees to vacate that part of their territory that fell within the state's boundaries. Now Georgia was anxious to expel the Cherokees from territory that the state wished to claim as its own.

The federal government provided land in Arkansas for the Cherokees, and a number decided to move there. But many Cherokees had no desire to leave their Eastern homeland. Following suggestions made by Jefferson (which he had hoped would lead to dissolution of the Indian communities), the Cherokees had rapidly developed practices and acquired technologies that were characteristic of European America. They adopted a written language, produced their own printed literature, established schools, created a constitutional government, built modern towns, and employed contemporary manufacturing and agricultural techniques.

They did exactly what they had been urged to do, and they resisted pressures to move.

Georgia became impatient. It permitted or encouraged its citizens to encroach upon Cherokee territory and harass the residents. In 1828, the year that Jackson was elected president, Georgia enacted legislation purporting to dissolve the Cherokee political structure and to distribute Cherokee territory to the surrounding Georgia counties. When gold was discovered that same year on Cherokee land, Georgia placed guards at the sites, from which they excluded the Cherokees who owned them.

Given the incontestable legal basis for the Cherokees' right to remain where they were, the Cherokee nation sought federal assistance against Georgia. Instead of providing it and honoring those legal commitments, Jackson secured passage of the Indian Removal Act in 1830. So the Cherokee nation sued Georgia in the US Supreme Court. But in *Cherokee Nation v. Georgia* (1831) a divided Court ruled that, as the Cherokee nation was neither a state (in the sense that Georgia and Massachusetts are states) nor a foreign nation, but only, in Chief Justice Marshall's terms, a "domestic dependent nation" within the United States, the Cherokee nation lacked "standing" under the Constitution to sue Georgia and the Court lacked jurisdiction to hear their grievance, regardless of its legal merits.

And the legal merits of the Cherokees' claim were undeniable. One might therefore have expected the Court to find a way to enforce the Cherokees nation's rights, perhaps by applying the Common Law maxim that no legal right lacks a remedy. The Court failed to do so.

That did not put an end to the matter. Georgia had also barred outsiders from visiting the Cherokees without the state's permission and had prosecuted several missionaries, who were friends of the Cherokees, for doing so. Samuel Worcester and others were convicted and sentenced to hard labor. As citizens of other states, however, the missionaries had standing to sue Georgia in the federal courts. In *Worcester v. Georgia* (1832) the Supreme Court ruled that Georgia's actions against the Cherokees (which included the legal basis for its prosecution of the mission-aries) violated the various guarantees that had earlier been cited by the Cherokee nation. The Court struck down Georgia's legislation against the Cherokees and nullified the missionaries' convictions.

The Supreme Court relied on the federal government to enforce its decisions, but Jackson did nothing to enforce *Worcester v. Georgia*. Jackson did not inter-fere with arrangements that eventually were made to free Worcester and his companions. But Indian Removal was another matter.

The Indian Removal Act required Indian consent before removal could law-fully occur. Some Cherokees agreed to relocate but most did not. In violation of the Act, Jackson ordered the army to force the remaining Cherokees out of their homeland and direct them to a designated sector of land beyond the Mississippi River (part of what would later become Oklahoma). The result was a thousand-mile march in the winter of 1838 on what came to be known as the "Trail of

Tears," during which four thousand of the fifteen thousand migrating Cherokees died, of starvation, disease, and exposure.

Other large Southeastern nations – the Choctaws, Creeks, Chickasaws, and Seminoles – were persuaded or forced to move. The migrations, involving tens of thousands of Native Americans, occurred mainly between 1831 and 1842. Most Indian nations went to lands that were to be reserved for them forever – but which later became states within which Native Americans lacked citizenship rights. Thus was more land made available for the expansion of a cotton-producing slave society.

The antebellum North was ambivalent about the color line. Northern states gradually ended slavery but many Northerners accepted the ideology and practices of white supremacy, ranging from school segregation to the exclusion of black workers from many types of work. Opposition to the western expansion of slavery, known as the "free soil" movement, did not generally include allowing free African Americans the right to live in western states or territories.

At the same time, the North resisted enforcement of the 1793 Fugitive Slave Act, both privately and officially. The Act authorized a person who claimed to own an escaped slave or persons acting on the supposed slave owner's behalf "to seize or arrest" the alleged escapee and present proof of ownership to a judge who, if satisfied, was to order removal of the alleged fugitive to the place from which they were supposed to have escaped. Although the Act did not stipulate the character of the judicial proceeding, it was widely interpreted to require no more than a summary hearing to determine whether a seized individual was to be treated as an escaped slave. This meant that a person held under the law might be denied the opportunity to rebut claims that were submitted on behalf of slave owners. Due process was effectively denied, although Amendment V of the Constitution declared that "[no] person shall be … deprived of life, liberty, or property, without due process of law," and the Constitution's Three-Fifths Clause made clear that slaves counted as persons.

Northern states enacted "personal liberty laws" that were intended in part to protect free black Northerners from being kidnapped and consigned to slavery without an opportunity to defend themselves. Personal liberty laws also expressed opposition to the idea of being required to support slavery, if not opposition to slavery itself. Some of the laws respected the federal Constitution by requiring due process in state courts – a fair opportunity for an alleged fugitive to rebut the claim; other laws prohibited state officials from participating in enforcement of the Fugitive Slave Law. Southerners resented such interference with the recovery of their most valuable property.

The Supreme Court may have thought it ended that controversy when in 1842 it decided *Prigg v. Pennsylvania*, which upheld the Fugitive Slave Act but agreed that state officials could not be required by federal law to aid its enforcement. Soon after, however, the congressional Compromise of 1850 amended the Fugitive Slave Act, which then violated the Constitution's due process requirement by explicitly barring testimony in the hearings on behalf of alleged fugitives and by rewarding officials who conducted the hearings a fee for ruling in favor of slave owners that was twice as large as the fee for ruling against them! The North–South conflict over the Fugitive Slave Act was by no means settled.

With the expansion of slavery, agitation for and against the institution increased greatly. A pro-slavery literature developed, offering positive justifications for the institution. Some argued that African Americans belonged to an inferior race – that they were docile, submissive, of low intelligence, lacking noble sentiments, with weak family relations, incapable of improvement or of prudent self-rule, incapable of competing with members of the white race, and in need of the discipline that masters provide. The new literature thus depicted African Americans as fitted for slavery, which provided them with reasonable work, leisure, and security. The literature assured its readers that black slaves showed no resentment of their inferior social position and were inclined to seek neither their own freedom nor closer relations with their white superiors.

Not all pro-slavery arguments were overtly racist. Some argued on the one hand that black slaves were better off than Northern wage workers, who lacked security and faced unemployment, begging, and starvation, and on the other hand that white workers benefitted from having jobs that the slavery-based economy made possible, as in the manufacture and shipping of cotton cloth and clothing. Some argued that the Northern political system was inherently unstable because political stability required class domination of an exploited subordinate class. Besides, it was said, the previous century's constitutional settlement committed the North to non-interference with slavery in the South. It was argued, finally, that the abolition of slavery would result in a bloody and devastating civil war or else inter-racial warfare, which would end with the elimination of either the black or the white race.

The system of chattel slavery in America was defended most notably by Thomas Ruffin of North Carolina in the case of *State v. Mann* (1830). Ruffin, a respected jurist, argued that the very nature of slavery requires that the slave-owner's control over his slave must be absolute and unlimited.

Part of the explanation for the growth of pro-slavery propaganda was the rise of anti-slavery agitation in America and abroad. Boston was a center of abolitionist activity. One of its most notorious practitioners was David Walker, a free African American. In 1829 Walker published his *Appeal to the Colored Citizens of the World,* which called upon black Americans to secure their own freedom, by force if necessary. Walker stressed the hypocrisy of those who embraced the Declaration of Independence and Christian values but failed to condemn slavery. His *Appeal* was circulated widely, even in the South, where attempts were made to suppress it. A price was put on Walker's head and he died in 1830 of uncertain causes.

Walker must have confirmed many Southern slave owners' fears of the Haitian example. Slave revolts were commonplace in the Americas, especially in the sugar islands of the Caribbean, where black slaves vastly outnumbered their white overlords. The most successful – and bloodiest – Caribbean slave revolt occurred in the French colony of Saint-Domingue, which began in 1791 and ended in 1804 with the establishment of the black republic of Haiti.

The US refused to support colonial independence movements in the Americas, partly in order to maintain good bargaining relations with Spain, whose colonial territories it coveted, and partly because the independence movements endorsed the abolition of slavery, which American political leaders rejected. The US aided French attempts to regain its former colony of Saint-Domingue and, after the French failed, America declined to recognize Haiti as an independent nation until 1862 (during the American Civil War).

Slave uprisings occurred in the US too. Some of the largest included the Stono Rebellion of 1739, one led by Gabriel Prosser in Virginia (1800), the German Coast uprising in Louisiana (1811), one led by Denmark Vesey in South Carolina (1822), and one led by Nat Turner in Virginia (1831). Slave revolts in the United States were smaller and less frequent than elsewhere in the Americas, because plantations and the ratio of black to white persons were smaller. Black resistance to slavery in America tended to consist of arson, poisoning, theft, feigning illness, and labor slow-downs.

Walker's *Appeal* was followed by the development of abolitionist organizations on a national scale. One of the most prominent white abolitionists was William Lloyd Garrison, who in 1831 established *The Liberator,* perhaps the most influential anti-slavery newspaper. Garrison also helped to found the American Anti-Slavery Society in 1832. Most of *The Liberator*'s subscribers were African Americans – as were many "conductors" on the Underground Railroad, which covertly and unlawfully helped fugitives make their way to Canada or to welcoming black communities in Boston, Massachusetts, and Rochester, New York. Like Walker, Garrison rejected "colonization" – the migration of black Americans to Africa. African Americans had as good a claim as any other non-indigenous people to remaining in America, which was their home. Reform called for liberation, not withdrawal or expulsion. (It also called, of course, for recognition of and respect for Native American claims – but that issue was rarely addressed, even by abolitionists.)

Discrimination against African Americans was widespread in the North, which was by no means uniformly sympathetic to abolitionism. Abolitionist speakers were often targets of physical as well as verbal attacks. African Americans, including former slaves who could report their own personal experiences, were prominent participants in the movement. They found racism within the abolitionist movement itself.

Given prevailing values, female abolitionists found it necessary to defend their right to act equally with men in the public sphere. Among the earliest notable women in the abolitionist movement were the Grimké sisters, who became outspoken advocates for women's rights along with abolition. Many leaders of the mid-nineteenth century women's rights movement began as abolitionists. One was Sojourner Truth, who addressed the 1851 Ohio Women's Rights Convention saying: "I have plowed, and planted, and gathered into barns, and no man could head me – and ain't I a woman? I could work as much and eat as much as a man (when I could get it) – and bear the lash as well – and ain't I a woman?"

The most prominent black abolitionist was Frederick Douglass, an escaped slave whose freedom was later purchased by some of his supporters. When called upon to speak in celebration of July 4 in 1852, he echoed David Walker:

> What to the American slave is your Fourth of July? ... To him your cele-
> bration is a sham; your boasted liberty an unholy license; your national
> greatness, swelling vanity; your sounds of rejoicing are empty and heartless;
> your shouts of liberty and equality, hollow mock; your prayers and hymns,
> your sermons and thanksgivings, with all your religious parade and solem-
> nity, are to him mere bombast, fraud, deception, impiety, and hypocrisy.

Douglass and Garrison worked closely together until the 1840s, when they disagreed about political strategy and the US Constitution. Garrison denounced the Constitution as a pro-slavery document ("a covenant with death, an agreement with hell"), regarded moral suasion as the means of reform, rejected conventional political action as acceptance of a system that was dominated by slave owners, and favored Northern secession from the Union in order to end its complicity with slavery. Douglass interpreted the Constitution in terms of its commitment to "establish Justice ... and secure the Blessings of Liberty to ourselves and our Posterity" and argued, with a few others, that slavery was incompatible with America's basic law. He rejected Garrison's secessionist proposal, which he thought would be tantamount to the abandonment of slaves. Our responsibility, he held, was to secure their freedom.

8

MORE LAND AND LABOR

During the middle of the nineteenth century two European countries provided the most newcomers to America. Between 1820 and 1860 one and a half million Germans came, many for religious or political freedom, as well as two million Irish Catholics. We will focus here on the Irish and two other groups who joined the US and whose histories are interwoven with the color line.

They came to a country that was expanding greatly in size. The Louisiana Purchase of 1803 had doubled America's territorial area, which now extended from the Atlantic Ocean to the Rocky Mountains. In 1845 the US took control by treaty of the Oregon Territory and in 1848 it acquired by war the northern half of Mexico, which together comprise the western portion (more than a third) of what is now the continental United States. Although those lands were populated, they were seen by many European Americans as theirs to take.

The Irish newcomers had first to escape starvation and disease at home and then to survive the "coffin ships" that carried them across the Atlantic. They were the most impoverished of voluntary immigrants. As many of them could not afford to travel beyond their ports of debarkation, they settled mainly in eastern port cities, to reside in the worst conditions of urban blight.

The English regarded Irish Catholics as uncivilized savages and contemptible papists, which influenced American views of Irish immigrants. Irish men were regarded as lazy drunks and Irish women as incessant breeders, suited for only the most dangerous and dirty jobs, the lowest-paid, low-skilled work.

Like some other European immigrants later in the nineteenth century, the whiteness credentials of Irish immigrants were questioned by some European Americans. But, like most of those later European immigrants, the Irish were capable of *becoming* white. They were welcomed by Democratic politicians whose influence in Northern cities enabled them to dispense patronage in the form of public sector jobs, and who could offer employment in exchange for electoral support. Many Irish men found jobs building railroads and canals (while many Irish women, most of whom came alone, found work in cotton mills or domestic service). The Democratic Party represented Southern slaveholding interests and many of their Irish beneficiaries absorbed the Democrats' racial attitudes. The newcomers' rejection of abolition may partly be explained by the fear that it would free African Americans to move North and compete with them for the low-status, low-paying jobs to which both groups were confined. The acquisition of these attitudes by Irish newcomers enabled them to become accepted as full-fledged (white) Americans. But it also divided them from their siblings in Ireland, who equated American racism with England's view of the Irish.

The Irish American experience may be compared with that of two other groups who joined America in mid-century: Mexicans and Chinese.

Inspired by the British colonies' successful war for independence, Spain's New World colonies rebelled, beginning early in the nineteenth century. Many of them looked to America for support, but were disappointed. The US, as we've noted, wished to remain on good terms with Spain, whose colonies it coveted. Also, American policy rejected the rebels' condemnation of slavery.

By 1825 all Spanish colonies in the Americas except Cuba and Puerto Rico had achieved independence, including Mexico in 1821. By then, Anglos from the US were settling in Mexico's northeastern region of Tejas. As the area was sparsely populated, the Mexican government initially welcomed all newcomers.

Anglos soon outnumbered Mexicans there, and many came to Tejas with their slaves. After Mexico abolished slavery in 1829, it banned further immigration from the US. That gave Anglo settlers a reason to seek the independence of Texas, which they regarded as achieved in 1836. The US annexed Texas in 1845 and then provoked a war with Mexico in order to secure even more of its territory.

To fight that war, the US Army recruited many Irish, German, and other recent Catholic immigrants. The contemptuous mistreatment by some American soldiers of Mexican civilians, including Catholic priests, led scores of the Catholic recruits to switch sides, forming the Saint Patrick's Battalion (the San Patricio Brigade), which fought with the Mexican Army against the US.

Under the 1848 Treaty of Guadalupe Hidalgo, which ended the war, the US acquired the northern half of Mexico's territory. The cession included what would become California, Nevada, Utah, most of Arizona, New Mexico and Colorado, and parts of Wyoming and Kansas – plus Texas, the independence of which Mexico had not previously recognized.

The treaty provided that the tens of thousands of Mexicans who resided in the ceded territory would become US citizens (unless they left or applied to retain their Mexican citizenship, which few did). Although they became US citizens, they did not enjoy equal rights under US law. For the next century Mexican Americans would be subjected to systematic discrimination. They were prevented from voting, segregated in schools and other public facilities, confined to menial work, and treated with contempt as "greasers." During the Great Depression of the 1930s, hundreds of thousands of Mexican Americans, including many US citizens, were treated as aliens and deported to Mexico.

Perhaps the Mexican Americans' greatest material loss was land – properties to which they had rights under Spanish and Mexican law. In two earlier treaties, concerning Louisiana (1803) and Florida (1821), the US had pledged to honor property rights under Mexican and Spanish law within the territories it was acquiring. Those promises were kept. The US made the same commitment in the Treaty of Guadalupe Hidalgo. That promise was broken.

Article 8 of the treaty said that Mexican citizens would retain their property rights regardless of their decisions concerning citizenship and residence. Article 10 emphasized the point by saying that land claims would be decided according to Mexican and Spanish law. (Legislation of the Mexican republic had validated the customary procedures of the prior two centuries.) Before the US Senate ratified the treaty, however, it deleted article 10. US negotiators then signed the Protocol of Queretaro, which committed America to respect Mexican land grants according to Mexican law. All three branches of the US government violated that commitment.

It happened first in California. After gold was discovered, California experienced a rapid inflow of fortune-seekers from America and other countries, including experienced miners from Mexico and South America. Because of the gold rush, land claims had special importance. California achieved statehood in 1850 and in 1851 Congress created the California Land Claims Commission, which established proof requirements that followed American rather than Mexican law. Deadlines, filing costs, and language barriers were additional obstacles for Mexican claimants, but the Commission's rules were all upheld by the US Supreme Court. As a result, many Mexican Americans lost land for which they had valid claims under Spanish and Mexican law.

In the early 1850s representatives of the federal government negotiated treaties with many California Indian communities, members of which had become US citizens under the treaty with Mexico. The communities agreed to exchange most of their California land for reservations plus aid in kind, such as livestock, clothing, and farm equipment. The US Senate rejected the treaties without informing the California Indians, and the treaties were not implemented. Indian land claims were adjudicated under California law and most Indian land went uncompensated into the public domain.

In 1854 Congress established the office of the Surveyor-General of New Mexico to deal with land claims in that territory. The agency received inadequate resources and adopted defective modes of operation. It favored first claimants, failed to notify other potentially affected parties, and imposed expensive, burdensome procedures for filing claims. Officials involved in the process often had conflicts of interest, many claimants were dishonest, and many claims were validated although they exceeded statutory limits. As a result, much land was lost by Mexican Americans who had valid grants.

In 1891 Congress replaced the Surveyor-General with a Court of Private Land Claims. But similar problems afflicted the new system. Federal courts disfavored community grants of common lands, needed by community members for grazing, hunting, fishing, quarrying, and the gathering of herbs. Altogether, of thirty-six million acres claimed by Mexican Americans, only three million were secured. Many Mexican Americans lost their economic independence. Thus the color brown was added to the non-white side of the color line.

Chinese immigrants were attracted by the prospects of work and perhaps riches, after gold was discovered in California in 1848. A few hundred Chinese had come earlier but most arrived between 1851 and 1882, when Congress stopped Chinese immigration. The 1880 US census counted one hundred and five thousand Chinese Americans – only 0.2% of the total US population of fifty million. Their impact was disproportionately greater.

Chinese men, intending to be sojourners rather than settlers, left families behind and came alone. Like many other immigrants, they fled difficult conditions brought by wars, floods, and heavy taxes. During the 1850s most of the Chinese immigrants went to the California gold fields. When the gold ran out, some found work in quartz mining. Many helped construct the western portion of the first transcontinental railroad during the 1860s. Consigned to dangerous work as well as lower wages than European Americans, they comprised up to 90% of the construction crew. They rebelled unsuccessfully against the discrimination they faced. Following the 1869 completion of the railroad, many returned to San Francisco for jobs in manufacturing, where they came to comprise half of the workforce. Some opened small businesses such as laundries (which were unknown in China). Many had been farmers in southern China and applied their expertise to draining swamps and marshes and constructing irrigation networks, laying the foundation for modern California agriculture.

But from early on they were harassed and worse. European American miners sought to evict them from the gold fields by threats and violence. To minimize their vulnerability, many Chinese worked in teams and on sites that others regarded as unproductive. Racial exclusion led them to develop "Chinatowns" in urban centers, such as San Francisco. But lynchings and pogroms forced them to abandon some towns entirely.

Chinese Americans also experienced discrimination under local, state, and federal law, which they challenged, sometimes successfully. In 1852, for example, the California legislature imposed a foreign miners' tax, which funded a major portion of the state's budget, until it was voided by a federal court under the Civil Rights Act of 1870. California's state constitution of 1879 prohibited the employment of Chinese by government agencies and private corporations, but the provision was nullified by the US Circuit Court of Appeals.

In 1855 the California legislature imposed a landing tax on those who brought Chinese to the state's ports. This was struck down by the California courts; but California courts were not always sympathetic. In the case of *People v. Hall*, the state Supreme Court ruled in 1854 that Chinese could not testify for or against white persons. The Court reached this conclusion by expansively reading statutes that excluded testimony from African Americans and Indians. The following passage from the Chief Justice's opinion suggests prevailing attitudes:

> The same rule which would admit [Chinese Americans] to testify, would admit them to all the equal rights of citizenship, and we might soon see them at the polls, in the jury box, upon the bench, and in our legislative halls.
>
> This is not a speculation which exists in the excited and over-heated imagination of the patriot and statesman, but it is an actual and present danger.
>
> The anomalous spectacle of a distinct people, living in our community, recognizing no laws of this State, except through necessity, bringing with them their prejudices and national feuds, in which they indulge in open violation of law; whose mendacity is proverbial; a race of people whom nature has marked inferior, and who are incapable of progress or intellectual development beyond a certain point, as their history has shown; differing in language, opinions, color, and physical conformation; between whom and ourselves nature has placed an impassable difference, is now presented, and for them is claimed, not only the right to swear away the life of a citizen, but the further privilege of participating with us in administering the affairs of our Government.

The Court's ruling meant that Chinese Americans would lack legal means to rectify most of the legal wrongs to which they were subjected.

Chinese Americans were frequently blamed for job shortages during economic crises. This led ultimately to the Chinese Exclusion Act of 1882 – the first federal enactment to bar from entry members of a specific ethnic group. This restriction was imposed at first for a limited term (ten years) because permanent exclusion would have violated the 1868 Burlingame Treaty between China and the United States, in which each nation promised freedom of travel and of residence within its borders for citizens of the other country.

The exclusion was expanded and intensified. Initially, for example, the Act permitted Chinese workers already in the US to reenter after traveling abroad (e.g., to visit family in China). Permission to reenter was voided by the Scott Act of 1888, which left some Chinese Americans who had left before that enactment unable to return as they had been promised. The Scott Act was upheld in the 1889 case of *Chae Chan Ping*. The Chinese Exclusion Act was renewed for another ten years in 1892 and was extended indefinitely ten years later. This led employers to look for other foreign workers who might be comparably exploited – a topic to which we shall soon return.

The US Supreme Court did not always rule against Chinese appellants. In *Yick Wo v. Hopkins*, the Court in 1886 perceived a violation of the fourteenth amendment beneath a superficially neutral law – a San Francisco ordinance that was applied in a systematically discriminatory manner against Chinese laundries. And in the 1898 case of *Wong Kim Ark*, the Court confirmed that the first clause of the fourteenth amendment, which conferred US citizenship on any person born in the United States, meant what it said. As a result, birthright citizenship was conferred on another group who were also classified officially as non-white (specifically, yellow) and treated as second-class citizens.

The reception and treatment of Mexican, Chinese, and (for a while) Irish newcomers confirmed and elaborated upon America's commitment to a system of racial stratification. Whiteness was a valuable property, an unearned passport to the "privilege" of decent treatment, including respect for whites' legal rights.

9

SECTIONAL CONFLICTS AND THE COLOR LINE

Until the Civil War began, Northern and Southern representatives in Congress continued to worry that their respective regions would be outvoted on crucial issues such as tariffs and how much of the newly acquired territory would be open to slavery. Attempts to limit slave territory did not generally signify a rejection of the color line. Many white persons in the increasingly crowded East wanted some land of their own in the West – and did not wish to share the territory with free African Americans. Northern business wanted to limit the number of new slave states and their impact on federal legislation.

Some measures seem intended to preserve the balance of power. In 1820, for example, Congress reached the Missouri Compromise, which banned slavery in new states and territories that lay north of the 36° 30' parallel, except for the new state of Missouri, which protruded above the compromise line but allowed slavery.

The issue was reopened after the Mexican War (1846–48) when the US acquired extensive territory from which several new states would presumably emerge. In addition, Texas, a recently annexed slave state, claimed land that lay north of the compromise line. And what was to be done about California, which straddled the 36° 30' parallel?

A compromise was reached in 1850: California would be admitted as a free state. Texas would give up its claim to territory north of the compromise line in return for the federal government's assuming the state's debt. To make the slave trade less visible to foreign visitors, slave auctions – the sale and purchase of human beings – would no longer be held in the District of Columbia, but part of the district would be returned to Virginia, where the slave trade could continue unimpeded. The remainder of the Mexican Cession (less California and Texas) would become the territories of New Mexico and Utah (each much larger than the state that later acquired its territorial name). "Popular sovereignty" was prescribed for those territories, which meant that slavery would be allowed in new states both north and south of the Missouri Compromise line, unless it was rejected by a vote of the residents. And, as we noted earlier, the 1793 Fugitive Slave Act was amended in 1850 so that its procedures much more strongly favored slaveholders' claims. The compromise seemed to favor the South.

The popular sovereignty provision guaranteed that conflicts over new states and territories would intensify. The Kansas-Nebraska Act of 1854 then expanded the area of conflict by prescribing popular sovereignty even to territories from which slavery had been banned by the Missouri Compromise of 1820. One result was "Bleeding Kansas" – deadly warfare between pro-slavery and anti-slavery groups who moved to Kansas in hopes of deciding the vote on slavery. The anti-slavery side prevailed, but Kansas was not admitted as a free state until 1861, after the Civil War had begun.

The Republican Party developed out of opposition to the Kansas-Nebraska Act. Lincoln noted at the time that the term "popular sovereignty" was misleading. It implied respect for self-government, but slavery violates that principle by subjecting those enslaved to the control of their masters.

The Fugitive Slave Act was resented more than ever in the North because the 1850 amendments more seriously threatened enslavement for persons who were claimed by slave owners, whether or not they had been slaves, and authorized federal marshals to conscript citizens to help slave owners seize and hold persons who were supposed to have escaped from slavery. During the 1850s, attempts were made in the courts and sometimes by force (in a few cases successfully) to free African Americans who had been seized as fugitives.

One court case is especially worth recalling because of the way its judicial opinion reflects color line ideology. In 1851 Thomas Sims was seized in Boston as a fugitive slave. While he was being held by federal marshals, lawyers petitioned the Supreme Judicial Court of Massachusetts to intervene and order Sims's release. The judge was Lemuel Shaw, long-serving and highly respected Chief Justice

Shaw denied the petition. In reaching his decision, Shaw held that the constitutionality of the Fugitive Slave Act had been settled in 1842 by the US Supreme Court's decision in *Prigg v. Pennsylvania*. His reasoning ignored the 1850 amendments which, as we have noted, violated due process rights by denying an alleged fugitive any opportunity to rebut the claim against him as well as by offering a monetary incentive for the hearing officer to rule in favor of the slave-owning claimant – constitutional defects that could easily determine the fate of someone like Thomas Sims.

Shaw was not content to leave matters there. He appended a long note to his opinion, defending the Fugitive Slave Clause of the US Constitution, which was not at issue in the case. Shaw argued that, without a commitment by the North to return escaped slaves, war would eventually break out between free states that harbored fugitives and slave states that wanted them back. Shaw argued, in effect, that inclusion of the clause was justified because it served the common good.

One problem with Shaw's reasoning is that Shaw, a learned man, presumably knew that war conditions benefit slaves by enabling them to escape their bondage and that this happened on a very large scale during the American War for Independence. (It would happen once again during the Civil War.) If Shaw had considered the interests of African Americans when weighing the pros and cons of including the Fugitive Slave Clause in the Constitution, the value of freedom for thousands of escaping slaves should have given him pause. Shaw reasoned as if the interests of African Americans needn't be considered along with the interests of white Americans.

The same position was taken a few years later by Chief Justice Taney of the US Supreme Court in deciding the 1857 case of *Dred Scott v. Sandford*. On the strength of well-established precedents, Scott had petitioned for his freedom from slavery and the freedom of his wife Harriet and their two children. Scott had been taken by his owner, John Emerson, a medical officer in the US Army, to Emerson's postings in territories from which Congress in 1820 had banned slavery. First separately and then together (after they married), Dred and Harriet Scott had resided in free territories for several years. Dr. Emerson died after the Scotts moved to Dr. Emerson's home in Missouri. The Scotts and their children then supposedly became the property of Dr. Emerson's widow, Irene Emerson. Dred Scott offered to purchase his family's freedom from Ms. Emerson, but she refused. Dred Scott then sued for their freedom in the Missouri courts.

Missouri was a slave state, but like other slave states it had consistently followed the principle that a slave is emancipated by being taken into free territory, and a jury accordingly decided for Scott. But Ms. Emerson appealed to the Missouri Supreme Court, which reversed its own precedents and overturned the lower court's decision.

By then Irene Emerson had moved away and assigned ownership of the Scotts to her brother John Sanford (whose name is misspelled in US Supreme Court records). As Sanford was a citizen of New York and the Scotts had been treated by the Missouri courts as citizens of that state, Dred Scott sued Sanford in federal court under the Diversity Clause of the US Constitution, which enables a citizen of one state to sue a citizen of another state in federal court. When he lost his case in the lower federal court, Scott appealed to the US Supreme Court.

It was an important case and each member of the divided Court submitted an opinion. The consensus was that Dred Scott could not sue Sanford in federal court because he was not a citizen of a state in the sense that was required under the Diversity Clause. The reason given was that African Americans could not be American citizens. According to Chief Justice Taney, when the US was founded all agreed that the descendants of Africans, whether enslaved or free, were "altogether unfit to associate with the white race, either in social or political relations, and so far inferior that they had no rights which the white man was bound to respect."

Even for the time, that was a shocking assertion. It went much further than the prevailing law of slavery which by then had placed limits on the behavior of slave owners towards their own slaves. Owners could be prosecuted in slave states for homicide and cruelty, which implied that African American slaves have rights that white men were bound to respect.

Chief Justice Taney misrepresented not only American law but also the surrounding history. He said, for example, that when the United States was founded no one questioned the subjugation of African Americans and their exclusion from the American political process. But it was no secret that many white as well as black Americans had campaigned against slavery when the US Constitution was drafted and ratified. Moreover, African Americans voted in several states prior to adoption of the Constitution.

The Declaration of Independence declared that "all men are created equal, that they are endowed by their Creator with certain unalienable rights, that among these are life, liberty and the pursuit of happiness." Taney argued that those who endorsed the document did not mean *all* men. He reasoned that some of the most distinguished signers of the Declaration were slaveholders, and to be a slaveholder is to act as if those who are enslaved lack rights to liberty and the pursuit of happiness. So, either those who signed the Declaration endorsed the principles as stated – as applicable to *all* men – but failed to live up to them, or the principles must be understood as inapplicable to African Americans. To suggest the former is unacceptable, Taney held, because it disparages those distinguished signers of the Declaration of Independence. It is better to deny that they violated their own principles than to admit that African Americans have rights that white persons are bound to respect.

The Supreme Court might reasonably have ended its decision-making in the case once it had decided that it lacked jurisdiction to hear Dred Scott's appeal. Instead, the Court went on to rule on issues that had not been raised by either party. It held, for example, that Congress lacked authority to ban slavery in a territory because that would violate a slaveholders' constitutional right to property by limiting where he might move with his slave. This ruling implied that all actions after 1789 that banned slavery in specified regions were constitutionally unsustainable. In Taney's view, the right to hold people as slaves and to take them where one wishes overrides the notion that African Americans have any enforceable rights.

Taney may have imagined that the Dred Scott decision would end political conflicts over the expansion of slavery, but that would have been wishful thinking. Opponents of slavery would never accept a political settlement that permitted slavery's unlimited expansion, and some abolitionists committed themselves fully to the anti-slavery cause.

That was true, for example, of John Brown, who was willing to use lethal force and risk his own life to free slaves. Brown was not alone. This was true of many who had been or were themselves enslaved.

Neither slaves nor abolitionists had originally introduced violence into disputes about slavery. Physical violence was essential to American slavery and was employed in its defense. Slaves were whipped, maimed, tortured, disabled, and killed in order to extract labor from them or their fellows and to keep them from running away. And to maintain such a system slave society supported an ideology that embraced cruelty and violence exercised with impunity. Lynching of free African Americans and abolitionists was encouraged and rarely prosecuted. Thus in 1837, for example, Elijah Lovejoy, an anti-slavery editor, was assaulted and killed and his press destroyed by a mob in Illinois. Lovejoy had protested the lynching of a free black man and the failure of officials to prosecute those responsible. And in 1856 the outspoken abolitionist Charles Sumner of Massachusetts was beaten senseless on the floor of the Senate by a congressman from South Carolina.

By contrast, the abolitionist movement was associated with nonviolence, as many who spoke out against slavery belonged to pacifist religious groups such as the Mennonites and Quakers.

But not all abolitionists embraced nonviolence. David Walker had called for a violent slave uprising if freedom was not granted peacefully. In the 1840s Henry David Thoreau refused to pay his Massachusetts poll tax in order to protest his state's cooperation with federal policies that supported slavery. As tax refusal is nonviolent, it might be thought that Thoreau was committed to nonviolence. In his famous lecture on civil disobedience, however, Thoreau suggested that violence can be justified against slavery as well as against other morally outrageous policies, such as America's war on Mexico. Thoreau later hailed John Brown's raid on Harpers Ferry.

John Brown became dedicated early on to ending slavery, but his notoriety was first established in "Bleeding Kansas." In 1856 Brown and his sons avenged the destruction of the anti-slavery center of Lawrence, Kansas, by executing several pro-slavery "border ruffians." Brown also developed a plan for inter-racial guerilla warfare against slavery. His idea was to take arms from the federal arsenal at Harpers Ferry and encourage slaves from the region to join his party in the nearby mountains, from which they would make forays to slave-populated plantations, some of whom would join the expanding abolitionist army. During the 1859 raid on Harpers Ferry, however, most of Brown's party became trapped, several were killed, and the rest, including Brown, were captured and then tried and executed for the raid, which had cost lives as well as federal property.

Brown and his party failed, but they reinforced slaveholders' view that their way of life was seriously threatened. And their bold action led some abolitionists who had been pacifists to think more sympathetically of violent measures against slavery.

10

CIVIL WAR AND RECONSTRUCTION

What was the Civil War about? In August 1862 Lincoln suggested that the war was not about slavery:

> My paramount object in this struggle is to save the Union. If I could save the Union without freeing any slave I would do it, and if I could save it by freeing all the slaves I would do it; and if I could save it by freeing some and leaving others alone I would also do that.

But it was unclear how to justify waging a war just to bring disaffected states back into the Union. Lincoln did not question the right of the disaffected British colonies eighty-five years earlier to break away from the British Empire. That precedent raised the question: why shouldn't disaffected states be allowed to leave the United States?

The Southern states that had formed a new confederation and initiated a war to secure their independence from the United States said clearly that they were defending slavery, including its territorially unlimited extension. In his second inaugural address (of March 1865), Lincoln acknowledged that slavery "was, somehow, the cause of the war."

Some Union supporters urged Lincoln early on to include as an aim of the war ending slavery, but others disagreed. Many Northerners feared greatly increased competition for jobs from African Americans if four million slaves were freed. Class divisions contributed in other ways to Northern political crises. In 1863 the Union followed the Confederacy's example by conscripting men into the army. But the system favored those who could afford to hire substitutes or pay to be exempted, which generated resentment that led to riots in Northern cities. In New York, the rioters' first targets were affluent members of the white community who had the wherewithal to avoid military service – but the rioters soon turned their lethal violence on the black community; they were angry at being forced to risk their lives for the emancipation of black slaves. The Union, however, had also begun to recruit black troops into the army, and they contributed significantly to Union military campaigns.

In December 1863 Lincoln issued a Proclamation of Amnesty and Reconstruction which offered to restore "all rights of property, except as to slaves," to those who had supported the Confederacy. After he was re-elected, in 1864, Lincoln actively supported the constitutional amendment that would abolish slavery throughout the United States.

Confederate war mobilization itself undermined slavery. As white Southerners left their homes to join the Confederate Army, some slaves were sent along to help with construction and do menial work. Other slaves replaced white Southerners who had worked in mines and factories. But most slaves were left to work on the plantations, and the more white Southerners joined the army, the fewer were left to oversee the slaves and conduct slave patrols. With reduced coercive control, slaves could more easily emancipate themselves.

And so they did. When Union forces got near, first scores, then hundreds, and finally thousands of slaves escaped to Union camps. Their presence created unexpected problems for the Union Army, however, for they required food and shelter. That gave Union officers good reason not only to use their labor but also to authorize their use of plantations that were abandoned by slave owners, where they could support themselves.

Here are some examples. When the Union Navy occupied Port Royal, South Carolina, in 1861, most white residents fled. The thousands of former slaves who remained rejected the idea of continuing cotton production and instead raised food crops for their own consumption. Port Royal became a self-governing, self-sufficient African American community.

In 1862, after the ten thousand acre plantation at Davis Bend, Mississippi, was abandoned by its owner, ex-slaves took it over. The following year General Grant authorized them to develop an autonomous community on the plantation, which became a well-run refuge for former slaves, who grew cotton profitably there for several years.

In 1865 General Sherman allocated the Sea Islands and coastal land south of Charleston to former slaves, each family to have forty acres and the loan of a mule. Forty thousand ex-slaves settled on the four hundred thousand acres that were available.

These examples clearly demonstrated the former slaves' ability to plan and regulate their work, support themselves, and participate in the governance of communities.

As Lincoln's December 1863 Proclamation of Amnesty and Reconstruction implied, reconstruction of the South would be required after a Union victory. But what did that mean? When Confederate states came under Union control, they required new governments. What conditions would they have to satisfy in order to be restored as full-fledged states of the Union, with representation in Congress?

Lincoln's proclamation required only that a "republican" state government be established by a number of persons who had been qualified to vote in the state prior to secession, who had since taken the new loyalty oath and had been faithful to it, and whose number totaled no less than 10% of the state's voters in the 1860 presidential election. Lincoln's proposal offered nothing to the former slaves, as it did not require that they be involved in a state's reconstruction.

After Lincoln's assassination, his presidential successor, Andrew Johnson, who was more sympathetic to the former slave owners than to the former slaves, offered even less. When states that had seceded came under Union control, provisional governments were established, controlled by white Southerners who sought to maintain a rigid racial hierarchy. Johnson allowed them to establish "Black Codes," which were designed to force freedmen on to plantations and into oppressive labor contracts.

Congress, now under "Radical" Republican leadership, rejected Johnson's policies and took over Reconstruction. Early in 1865 Congress had proposed Amendment Thirteen, abolishing slavery, which was ratified by the end of the year. In 1866 Congress enacted, over Johnson's veto, the first Civil Rights Act, which prohibited race discrimination in courts and contracts and conferred citizenship on all persons born in the US (thus reversing the principal ruling of the Dred Scott case). Congress also renewed the Freedmen's Bureau so that it could continue to provide emergency relief for white as well as black Southerners.

In 1867 Congress established military districts in the former Confederacy and laid down conditions for a state to regain representation in Congress. These included universal male suffrage – which meant that African American men could vote – and acceptance of the Fourteenth Amendment – which constitutionalized provisions of the 1866 Civil Rights Act and required that states provide equal protection to persons under their jurisdiction. In 1869 Congress proposed, and in 1870 the states ratified, the Fifteenth Amendment, which prohibited restrictions on voting rights based on race or previous condition of servitude. Congressional legislation supporting Reconstruction also included the 1875 Civil Rights Act, which required equal access to public accommodations, as well as laws prohibiting interference with African Americans' exercise of their civil rights, such as voting.

Under Congressional Reconstruction former slaves voted and were elected to public office. Southern states adopted new constitutions that satisfied the conditions laid down by Congress. The Freedmen's Bureau negotiated and enforced labor contracts and helped to create public schools and hospitals where none had previously existed.

Reconstruction was violently challenged. Coercion and terror, often organized by groups such as the Ku Klux Klan, Knights of the White Camelia, the White League, and the Red Shirts, were widely used to prevent the political and economic independence of African Americans or punish them for it. Hundreds of former slaves and their white allies were killed, many more were beaten, and as a consequence many fled the South.

In the early 1870s the Union Army showed that it could effectively combat such terrorist organizations. But those efforts were not continued, as they were thought by leading Republicans to be politically unsustainable. That decision foreshadowed the end of Reconstruction.

To provide a fuller picture of Reconstruction, we must go back again to 1865. At the war's end, the South was in disrepair. Four million persons had formally gained freedom but lacked secure means of subsistence and faced uncertain futures. Many searched for loved ones from whom they had been torn by past actions of slave owners. Revival of the South's economy required a new labor system. What would that be like?

The former slaves made clear what they wanted. While some migrated to cities and some left the South entirely, the vast majority remained in the rural South, which was home. Those who stayed understood freedom, which they had supposedly achieved, to mean social and economic independence and that this required a share of land that was capable of supporting a family.

It was a reasonable demand. On the one hand, former slaves had good moral claims for reparations. They had suffered the constraints, indignity, brutality, maiming, and suffering that chattel slavery imposed. Their coerced and uncompensated labor had largely built and run the profitable plantations and had contributed substantially to the South's economy as a whole. They had good claims to a substantial portion of the properties they had created and worked. The former slaves made the point and renewed their appeals, or demands, time and again. At the same time, political reconstruction of the South required the economic independence of its ordinary citizens from the former slaveholders, and that required a more equitable distribution of Southern land.

Could the former slaves cope with so much independence? The South's previously booming economy was built on African Americans' multi-faceted labor and established their productivity, while their successfully self-governing communities during the Civil War proved their administrative and organizational skills.

If the distribution of modest lots to ex-slaves was to be part of Reconstruction, how could it be achieved? The Freedmen's Bureau had gained control of more than 850,000 acres of abandoned land. Authorized by federal law to rent such land in forty acre lots, for eventual sale, it allocated some to former slaves. In 1865 Thaddeus Stevens, a leading Republican congressman, proposed that the federal government confiscate four hundred million acres that were owned by the wealthiest 10% of Southern landowners. Forty acres would be allocated to each adult freedman. The remaining 90% of the land seized would be sold in lots of up to five hundred acres, proceeds from which would fund pensions for Union veterans, compensation to loyal unionists for property losses in the war, and retirement of the national debt.

What Thaddeus Stevens proposed included land reform. In the post-Civil War South land reform would have had a political as well as an economic function. It would have enabled Southerners to replace a rigid hierarchy with social mobility and democracy. Of course, more than a plot of land is required for land reform to work. Farmers require an initial stake of supplies, equipment, and (as General Sherman recognized in his Field Order 15) the use of draft animals. They require credit, they must be able to purchase supplies, and they must have outlets for their surplus. They must not be subjected to systematic violence and cheating. In short, they require protection by the effective rule of non-discriminatory law. The redistribution of land was no panacea, but it was a necessary component of Southern reconstruction.

It is unclear how many white policy-makers considered the possibility that those who had been enslaved had a right to a modest plot of land or any other form of compensation. Before the Civil War, it was assumed that slave owners would be compensated if slavery was abolished and they lost their most valuable property.

In any case, land reform was never endorsed by most policy-makers, many of whom believed that abolition and universal manhood suffrage would suffice to reform Southern society. Land reform was opposed by Northern investors, who wished to restore large-scale Southern agriculture. Except for Radical Republicans like Stevens, Union leaders believed that the former slaves should become wage workers or tenant farmers.

Some Union policy-makers even condemned programs designed to aid ex slaves. They held that it would hurt them to be given land, for which they needed to learn to work and save. Some maintained that emergency relief through the Freedmen's Bureau would make them dependent upon government support. President Johnson argued that the Bureau's relief efforts discriminated against the white community, even though the Bureau served both communities.

Thaddeus Stevens' proposal was rejected by Congress in 1866. Land reform did not happen. Let's now consider what actually did happen.

The former slaves had been led to understand that the lands they had been allocated during the Civil War would remain theirs. President Johnson disagreed. He had been a bitter opponent of the Southern landed aristocracy but, hating black independence even more, he ordered the return of land to its previous owners. Freedmen appealed, to no avail, and the army removed them by force. In many cases, legal title to the land had never been passed to the freedmen.

Most of the land near Port Royal that slaves had been allowed to take over was auctioned off by government agents. The Davis Bend plantation was returned to the Davis family. Land that had been acquired by the government for non-payment of taxes or because it had been abandoned was auctioned off. As a result, relatively few freedmen acquired land of their own. And those who managed to become independent farmers faced violent hostility from white Southerners.

Planters wanted the former slaves to labor for them. White Southerners were generally determined to prevent the freedmen from achieving independence and political, economic, or social equality. Southern banks refused credit to freedmen, and property owners sold land to white persons for half the price offered by black persons, in order to ensure that the land would not come under black ownership.

These developments guaranteed that a meaningful reconstruction of the former slave states would not occur. So long as wealthy planters retained most of the land and freedmen were obliged to work it for them, the planters would maintain economic and political dominance.

The federal courts did not help. They could not by themselves have ensured that African Americans' civil rights would be respected, but judicial decisions prevented their full enforcement.

Consider, for example, the *Slaughterhouse Cases* of 1873. Although the dispute concerned economic monopolies, not the civil rights of African Americans, it gave the Supreme Court an occasion to interpret the new constitutional amendments which the complainants invoked. The Fourteenth Amendment explicitly authorized Congress to enforce its provisions. In ruling that the Amendment did not authorize federal enforcement of civil rights, the Court undermined one of the Fourteenth Amendment's central aims.

The Amendment declared that: "No state shall [for example] deny to any person within its jurisdiction the equal protection of the laws." In several cases, the Court held that such provisions concern only "state action" – actions of governments rather than private citizens. This meant that the federal government could not prosecute private individuals for preventing African Americans from exercising their civil rights. Given that ruling, in the *Civil Rights Cases* of 1883 the Court nullified central provisions of the Civil Rights Act of 1875. It held that Congress lacked the authority to regulate privately owned public accommodations, because the acts of inns, theaters, and railroads, when they are privately owned, are not state actions.

In dissent, Justice Harlan observed that state and federal courts had consistently treated inns, theaters, and railroads as performing public functions and as subject to regulation, which meant that their acts were tantamount to state action. The Court's contrary ruling meant that eighty-one years would pass before Congress would effectively legislate against racial discrimination in public accommodations.

In 1876 an electoral crisis followed disputed elections in Florida, Louisiana, and South Carolina. The stalemate was ended by the Hayes-Tilden agreement of 1877. In exchange for the assignment of electoral votes to the Republican presidential candidate, Rutherford Hayes, it was agreed that federal troops would be withdrawn from the South. Federal suppression of organized terror and supervision of Southern elections were ended.

After the Court eviscerated the 1875 Civil Rights Act, Congress ceased trying to ensure that African Americans could enjoy the rights that they were supposedly guaranteed by the amended Constitution. Its efforts had largely been frustrated and its attention turned to other matters.

Federal law might assert that black individuals had basic rights that were equal to those enjoyed by white individuals. But in fact their rights could not be exercised because they could not be enforced. Active federal intervention, including military force, was required to achieve some measure of democracy and the rule of law, but the South resented and the North was unenthusiastic about that intervention. When the federal government ended its enforcement of Reconstruction reforms, most of them, save the formal end to chattel slavery, were reversed.

Let's take stock. During the seventeenth century Southern colonies created the brutal system of racial exploitation that we know as chattel slavery. A century later the newly independent United States resolved to protect that system. The abolition of slavery signified a major shift in American law and policy, which Congressional Reconstruction sought to expand. But Reconstruction was aborted. Although America committed itself to civil rights for African Americans, it declined to enforce those rights. Its policies fell drastically short of its promises and constitutional pretensions. Freedmen were betrayed and a way was opened for a new system of racial subjugation.

Having the opportunity to end or significantly lessen America's commitment to white supremacy, those who held the levers of power declined to do so. America would continue to privilege what the dominant segments of society regarded as whiteness and to subordinate people of color.

11

REDEMPTION AND JIM CROW

During Reconstruction African Americans voted and were elected to public office, new state constitutions were established, and public schooling was begun. But Reconstruction was brief and its reforms were reversible. Before long, the Democratic Party regained control of all Southern state governments through the use of force, electoral fraud, and the sheer number of those who remained committed to the color line.

In 1879 the Supreme Court in *Strauder v. Virginia* ruled against the explicit exclusion of black men from juries. Thereafter, white Southern lawmakers took the precaution of using "color-blind" laws in order to exclude African Americans. Jury service was generally limited to those who were registered to vote, so excluding blacks from voter rolls also kept them off juries. The "color-blind" strategy worked: with rare exceptions, the federal courts accepted any legal arrangements to subordinate people of color as long as the language used was superficially neutral. (*Yick Wo v. Hopkins*, noted earlier, is one of the rare exceptions of this period in which the Supreme Court looked at facts beyond the statutory language.) White supremacists enacted laws and amended state constitutions with the explicit intention of disfranchising African Americans.

In *Williams v. Mississippi*, for example, the Supreme Court in 1898 upheld conditions for voter registration such as timely payment of the poll tax and the literacy test because they formally applied to all voters.

The terms of the poll tax ensured that the less affluent would be excluded. It was extremely burdensome for poor citizens, and the burden was magnified by the expense and difficulty of travel to offices at which the tax could be paid – offices that might have very limited hours of operation – as well as by the requirement that poll tax payments cover all past years of potential qualification. As expected, the vast majority of black men could not meet all of those conditions and they lost the right to vote.

The poll tax also disfranchised many poor white Southerners, but this effect was not unwelcome to all Southern lawmakers. If state lawmakers wished to allow poor whites to vote, however, they would add a "grandfather clause," which enfranchised anyone who had been qualified to vote before the Civil War as well as their descendants: that would enfranchise many white Southerners, but very few black Southerners.

The literacy test worked differently, enabling voting registrars to exclude whoever they disfavored. Applicants might be asked to explain some clause of the state's constitution, for example, and registrars had the unqualified authority to decide whether an interpretation was correct. White voting registrars were rarely satisfied with African Americans' performance, however good it might in fact be.

Voters could also be disqualified by restrictive residency requirements and by having had a criminal conviction (within a legal system that was grossly biased against its black subjects). The intended effect of these various legal devices was achieved: by 1900 the number of black registered voters in the Old South was reduced to a small fraction of what it had reached in the 1870s.

Many Southern states also adopted "white primaries," which barred non-white citizens from voting in primary elections. Because the primaries determined the nominees of political parties, which were not official state agencies, the federal courts regarded the exclusion of black voters from the primaries as private discrimination and thus no violation of African Americans' civil rights. This meant that black citizens of states with white primaries had no voice in determining candidates for public office. Once the Democrats had regained single-party control of the South, elections were effectively decided when candidates were selected.

And so the South was "redeemed": its commitment to white supremacy was institutionalized and the domination of plantation owners was reaffirmed.

As noted, most former slaves remained in the South and continued in agricultural work. Chattel slavery was formally prohibited but it was nonetheless possible for large landowners to develop a system of unfree labor. Freedmen who stayed in the rural South worked the land as wage laborers, as tenants who paid a set rent for use of a plot of land, or as sharecroppers on a plantation. More became tenant farmers than farm laborers but most became sharecroppers.

Under a sharecropping system, the landowner (who might be the freedman's former owner) would provide not only the land but also tools and farm animals. In exchange, the landowner held an enforceable claim to a substantial portion of the resulting crop or of the income from it. Very often the sharecropper would be obliged to purchase seeds and other necessities such as food and clothing from the landowner's store. As the landowner controlled the accounting and set both the prices his store charged (very high) and the value of the crop (very low), the sharecropper was likely to be told each year that he was in debt to the landowner.

Within the violently enforced system, sharecroppers could not safely challenge a landowner's accounting, even if clearly fraudulent, and as a result became prisoners of perpetual debt.

Another component of the Jim Crow labor system was convict leasing. Jailed or imprisoned persons would be hired out or leased to work on farms, railroads, mines, and logging sites. The state or local governing body would be paid by the employer for the convicts' services; leased out convict workers would not get paid. Sheriffs and courts would charge prisoners for arresting, prosecuting, convicting, and jailing them, and the fees would be converted into additional time to be served over and above whatever sentence was judicially imposed. Convict leasing became a major source of revenue for Southern states and a very low-cost source of labor for employers. When demand for convict workers rose, law enforcement officials would increase the supply by applying vagrancy and other laws – or, quite often, by misapplying them.

Leasing could be short- or long-term and convicts might be returned to their cells at night or housed by the private employers. Conditions of work could be horrific. Prisoners were provided with minimal food, shelter, or medical care, and many died on the job, to be buried near work sites. Convict leasing involved thousands of prisoners, many of whom were guilty of minor offenses – or of no offense at all.

The last third of the nineteenth century was also a period of unprecedented racial violence. With the abolition of slavery, African Americans were no longer private property, which meant that killing or injuring an African American did not require paying compensation to the owner. Thousands of African Americans were lynched between 1865 and 1930 – most frequently from 1865 to 1870 (resisting Reconstruction) and during the 1890s (establishing Jim Crow), when a lynching occurred every two or three days. Victims were often tortured and dismembered prior to being killed.

Many lynchings were public and some were publicized in advance. Photographs were taken at such events, with identifiable participants shown facing the camera, standing before one or more hanging black bodies or a charred black corpse. The photographs were printed as postcards and sent through the US mail. There was little need for secrecy, as violence against black men and women could be performed with impunity. Under Jim Crow, public officials were not much concerned about the murder or rape of an African American, and local officials themselves would sometimes participate. Officials who tried to prevent or prosecute lynchings would usually suffer sanctions such as defeat in the next election. If lynchers were prosecuted, they would be acquitted by all-white juries, however strong the evidence against them. Racist appeals made in their defense would be permitted by law or by judicial rulings.

Some of this was no doubt an expression of race hatred, nurtured by the culture of a slave society and intensified by the racist propaganda of the period. The violence may also have expressed a desire by some white persons to assert and reinforce their privileged position in a racially hierarchical system. But it also helped to consolidate and enforce the new system of unfree labor. The subordination of African Americans required constantly reminding them of their vulnerability.

For decades, African Americans and their allies campaigned unsuccessfully for federal legislation against lynching. During the twentieth century, anti-lynching bills were proposed but never made it through both houses of Congress. Given their control of elections in the South, Southern incumbents had disproportionate influence in Congress: their secure seats gave them enhanced seniority and chairmanships of congressional committees. National politicians such as the two presidents Roosevelt refrained from supporting civil rights reforms for fear of alienating Southern Democrats, whose votes were crucial to the national party's electoral strength. And many politicians wholeheartedly endorsed Jim Crow. Woodrow Wilson, for example, embraced white supremacy and imposed segregation in the federal bureaucracy.

Violence against black men and women was not limited to assaults on individuals or small groups. It included *pogroms* – attacks on entire black communities, especially politically independent or prosperous black communities, and on farmer or labor groups that organized collective resistance to Jim Crow practices. Examples of the former were the Wilmington Insurrection of 1898, which displaced an elected local government in North Carolina, and the Tulsa "race riot" of 1921, which destroyed a thriving black community in Oklahoma. An example of the latter was the Elaine Massacre of 1919, which began with an attack on a meeting of Arkansas sharecroppers who were organizing a union to seek fairer settlements from planters.

By the dawn of the twentieth century, political power was securely restored to a small class of economically dominant landowners and lynching became less frequent. Its primary political function was no longer to consolidate Jim Crow but to maintain it.

One of the most poignant illustrations of the negligible value placed on black lives under Jim Crow is the Tuskegee study undertaken in Alabama by the US Public Health Service to trace the effects of untreated syphilis on African American males. As a well-known Norwegian study had already determined the course of untreated syphilis in men, there was no scientific need for the Tuskegee study – unless one assumed there were relevant biological differences between black and white men, for which there was no scientific evidence. For the Tuskegee study, hundreds of black sharecroppers were recruited, including many who were diagnosed with the disease. They were offered free medical care and other benefits but they were not informed of the purpose of the program or of their diagnoses. When the study began in 1932, medical science lacked an effective treatment for syphilis. But when it was determined, by 1947, that penicillin could cure the disease, it was withheld from those in the study who were known to have syphilis; they were also prevented from getting treatment elsewhere. The study continued for another twenty-five years, until it was revealed by a "whistle-blower" to the press.

Dr. John Heller of the Public Health Service, who headed the study when the decision was made not to use penicillin, was reported to have said when interviewed that the men being studied "were subjects, not patients; clinical material, not sick people."

Thus Jim Crow went well beyond racial segregation. It was a system of subordination and exploitation maintained by racist ideology and terror. Black and white families did reside in separate neighborhoods and used separate facilities, but they were not otherwise separated. Many white families employed black domestic servants (one of the few job categories open to black women) who cleaned and cooked for the families and nurtured their children (as under chattel slavery). Many companies employed both black and white workers in close proximity, but with black workers confined to menial, less skilled, lower paid positions (although black workers had performed highly skilled work under slavery).

Separate facilities were rarely if ever equal. When white supremacists regained control of the South, they reduced public spending, revenue for which came mainly from property taxes. Under Jim Crow, services and facilities for African Americans were systematically underfunded, when they were provided at all. This meant that Jim Crow accommodations almost always violated the "separate but equal" requirement that was laid down in 1896 by the Supreme Court in *Plessy v. Ferguson*.

The point is more general and more damning: Jim Crow involved major, continuing *violations* of law, including Southern law. Consider the rare prosecutions of lynchers. No cases were dismissed on the ground that the law did not prohibit the deliberate, unprovoked killing of African Americans. In the service of white supremacy, public officials systematically violated their own laws and failed to apply laws they were charged with enforcing. Those conditions were well known to public officials outside the South, including the federal government. For people of color under Jim Crow, the rule of law was inaccessible.

Indeed, Jim Crow was by no means confined to the South. Systematic discrimination against African Americans and other people of color had been well established in the North long before the abolition of slavery, and residential segregation became more extreme and, along with school segregation, more deeply entrenched in the North than in the South.

The sentiments expressed in 1852 by Frederick Douglass seem applicable to Jim Crow and worth repeating here:

> What to the [African American] is your Fourth of July? … To him your celebration is a sham; your boasted liberty an unholy license; your national greatness, swelling vanity; your sounds of rejoicing are empty and heartless; your shouts of liberty and equality, hollow mock; your prayers and hymns, your sermons and thanksgivings, with all your religious parade and solemnity, are to him mere bombast, fraud, deception, impiety, and hypocrisy.

12

WESTERN INDIANS

The Louisiana Purchase of 1803, the 1846 acquisition of the Oregon Territory, and the Mexican Cession of 1848 greatly expanded US territorial claims, which now extended across the North American continent from the Atlantic to the Pacific Ocean. Most of the added territory was populated by Indian nations that regarded the land as theirs. Most Americans regarded the indigenous peoples as troublesome squatters, or worse.

Official negotiations with California Indians in the early 1850s revealed once again that indigenous groups were prepared to share the land on reasonable terms. They wished to preserve their sacred sites, freedom of movement, governance over territory they retained and their traditional ways of life, or their own choice as to what new way of life to adopt.

Chief Joseph of the Nez Perce put the matter this way:

> We only ask an even chance to live as other men live. We ask to be recognized as men. We ask that the same law shall work alike on all men. If the Indian breaks the law, punish him by the law. If the white man breaks the law, punish him also.
>
> Let me be a free man – free to travel, free to stop, free to work, free to trade where I choose, free to choose my own teachers, free to follow the religion of my fathers, free to think and talk and act for myself – and I will obey every law, or submit to the penalty.

Such reasonable conditions clashed with prevailing American attitudes. American policy-makers took for granted that Native Americans would be much better off if their religions and ways of life were replaced by Christianity and European American culture. They believed that Native Americans had much more land than they needed and should vacate – or be expelled from – land that white settlers wanted and white entrepreneurs were eager to exploit. They felt justified in imposing the changes they desired and dispossessing Indians whenever it was politically feasible to do so. By the end of the nineteenth century, Indian nations of the western regions were either persuaded or, more often, forced to cede most of the territory they reasonably understood to be theirs, and were confined to much smaller reservations. Many Indian children were forcibly taken from their parents to distant schools, which coercively barred Indian languages, dress, and practices.

Sitting Bull represented the Hunkpapa Sioux perspective in the following terms:

> We were free to come and go, and to live in our own way. But white men, who belong to another land, have come upon us, and are forcing us to live according to their ideas. That is an injustice; we have never dreamed of making white men live as we live.
>
> White men like to dig in the ground for their food. My people prefer to hunt the buffalo as their fathers did. White men like to stay in one place. My people want to move their tepees here and there to the different hunting grounds. The life of white men is slavery. They are prisoners in towns or farms. The life my people want is a life of freedom.

Although in 1871 Congress officially declared an end to treaty-making with Indian nations, the United States continued to conclude treaties with the indigenous peoples of California, the Great Plains, America's new Southwest, and its new Northwest. The US pledged annuities or comparable benefits in exchange for ceded lands and also pledged that the lands retained by the Indian nations were theirs forever. Few of those promises were kept.

Here, very briefly, is what transpired. The 1848 discovery of gold in California led very quickly to an influx of miners, prospectors, and settlers. Indians of the region were decimated by genocidal violence, disease, and starvation. Laws that promised apprenticeships were used to enslave Indians. Overwhelmed, the Indian nations of California all but disappeared.

In the Oregon territory, fur traders and Indians coexisted peacefully until Congress in 1850 opened the region to homesteading without regard to Indian land rights. Native Americans resisted the encroachments until 1858, when they suffered decisive defeats at the battles of Spokane Plains and Four Lakes. Indians of the region were then confined to reservations.

Conflict in the New Mexico territory had begun in 1846 when Apaches resisted encroachments on their land by miners and the US Army. After protracted hostilities, in 1876 Chiricahua Apaches were consigned to a barren reservation in Southeastern Arizona. Many refused to go, escaped, and continued hostilities. When the Apache Wars ended in 1886, indigenous survivors were exiled to reservations in distant parts of the country.

In 1851 the US Army began a campaign to control the Navajo in New Mexico. Hostilities reached a crucial point in the early 1860s when a volunteer contingent led by Kit Carson destroyed Navajo sheep, crops, wells, orchards, and housing. Thousands of Navajo were then forced on a Long Walk, of three hundred and fifty miles, on which they suffered extreme abuse, to the desolate reservation of Bosque Redondo. An 1868 treaty enabled the Navajo to return to a much smaller segment of their original territory, where they did not receive the livestock and supplies they had been promised.

At mid-century, much of the Louisiana Territory, including the Great Plains, remained (in official terms) politically "unorganized." But crowding and land-hunger in the East combined with the Gold Rush led to increasing numbers of white settlers crossing the Plains through Indian territory, mainly in wagon trains on the Santa Fe and Oregon Trails. In 1851 the federal government began negotiating with Indian nations of the region, such as the Cheyenne and Sioux, which resulted in the first Fort Laramie Treaty. That agreement divided the Plains into separate districts for the several Indian nations, which included their respective hunting grounds. The Indian communities pledged safe passage for the migrants and the government pledged annuities for ceded lands and compensation for damages they might suffer.

The government did not keep its promises. Before long, from Kansas in 1861 to Wyoming in 1890, seven states were established on land that the United States had guaranteed to the Indian nations forever.

In 1858 gold was found in Colorado. The resulting gold rush and unlawful settlements on guaranteed Indian land led to further negotiations with affected Indian communities. The 1861 Treaty of Fort Wise, signed by several Cheyenne and Arapaho chiefs, ceded more than 90% of the two nations' original reserve. Some Cheyenne rejected the treaty and refused to leave ceded lands. In 1864 US Army units attacked Cheyenne camps, killing friendly chiefs. Cheyenne retaliated, leading to further hostilities. Seeking peace, Black Kettle and White Antelope, with a large band of Cheyenne and Arapaho, went to Fort Lyon and were told to camp nearby along Sand Creek. While most of their warriors were away hunting, the camp was attacked by hundreds of Colorado volunteer militia. Twenty or thirty warriors and scores of women and children were massacred. This led to further retaliation raids by disaffected Cheyenne on settlers and properties, such as stagecoach stations and trains.

In 1864 the Bozeman Trail was established through Indian country in Wyoming and Montana. This led to warfare between the US Army and Indians of the region. The army established a chain of forts along the trail, but Indian resistance discouraged its use by civilians. Under the second Fort Laramie Treaty, of 1868, the army agreed to abandon the forts and reaffirmed security for the Indian communities and their hunting grounds.

With completion of the first transcontinental railroad in 1869, migrants heading west had less need for a wagon trail. But that did not end conflict in the region, which includes the Black Hills – sacred to the Sioux and guaranteed to them by the federal government. In 1874 Lieutenant Colonel George Armstrong Custer led a large army contingent into the area to seek gold and locate a new fort. A gold rush followed, as did war, including Custer's defeat at the Little Big Horn by Sioux under Sitting Bull.

Custer's expedition had followed an official policy of violating commitments to the Indians, which complemented the strategy of destroying the Plains Indians' main food supply. Beginning in 1872, the army promoted the slaughter of buffalo. At first only hides were taken and the buffalo carcasses were simply left to rot. Later, the bones were also collected, for they had industrial uses. Thirty million buffalo were killed, leaving a thousand buffalo survivors.

The army pursued the Sioux and forced a large number onto reservations. Sitting Bull led his band into Canada, but the Canadian government would not permit them to settle there. In 1881 Sitting Bull and his band returned to the US, and he was confined in the Standing Rock reservation.

In 1889 the Ghost Dance movement was revived in the Northern Plains. A spiritual phenomenon reflecting the great losses Indians had experienced, it created anxiety among white observers, who did not trouble to understand its significance. Their reaction led to the arrest and killing of Sitting Bull (who was not involved in the Ghost Dance movement) and the flight of Ghost Dancers, who were pursued by the army. A peaceful band of Indians under Big Foot surrendered at Wounded Knee, where they arranged to be disarmed. During that process an altercation led to the massacre of Big Foot's band (the Wounded Knee Massacre of 1890), which many view as the end of the ethnic cleansing that is known as the Plains Wars.

In 1887 Congress had enacted the Dawes (Allotment) Act, which provided for the dismemberment of Indian reservations. Plots of land were to be carved out of Indian territories and assigned to Indian families or individuals. Congress assumed that Indians would be better off liberated from tribal life, working small farms of their own. It seems no accident, however, that allotments to Indians under the Dawes Act left most of the originally reserved land available for settlement by European Americans. As Congress later acknowledged, some Indian nations were extinguished by the program. Indian landholdings in the US decreased from one hundred and thirty-eight million to forty-eight million acres.

Twenty million acres of the allotments were on semi-arid land that was unsuitable for farming. That made little difference, as those receiving the allotments could not have farmed them, had they wanted to. The government provided only ten dollars per allotment to cover start-up costs for the purchase of tools, equipment, supplies, and other necessities. The system was bound and perhaps designed to fail.

By the turn of the century, the American Indian population had declined to its lowest level since colonization began – about a quarter of a million. It looked as if American Indian policy was soon to achieve its apparent aim – the elimination of bothersome indigenous nations and their territorial rights.

13

CLOSING THE DOOR

The decennial census revealed that America's population expanded greatly during its first 130 years – from four million in 1790 to one hundred and six million in 1920. More than a third of the increase was due directly to immigration, almost all of the migrants coming from Europe. Many were impelled by poverty or persecution and were drawn by the prospect of work and visions of freedom.

American industry grew rapidly following the Civil War, and workers were actively recruited abroad. Employers wanted a surplus of workers on hand to keep wages down through competition for jobs. They also sought to employ workers from countries with existing antagonisms, so as to lessen the risk of unified labor action for better wages and conditions. They had reason for concern.

Factories and railroads were unregulated and much of the work was exceedingly dangerous. Child labor was widespread. One of the most devastating events was the 1911 Triangle Shirtwaist Fire in New York City which took the lives of one hundred and forty-six clothing workers, mostly young immigrant women. The factory occupied the eighth, ninth, and tenth floors of a building in lower Manhattan. It lacked a fire alarm, and one of the two exit doors was locked. Once the fire began, the stairs and elevators became unusable, and the fire escape collapsed. The fire company's ladder proved too short to reach those who were trapped. Eyewitnesses helplessly watched as a number of the trapped workers escaped from the fire by jumping to their deaths on the sidewalks below.

It is no wonder, then, that labor militancy developed, as did industrial unions and bitter strikes, which were fought, with sometimes lethal force, by police, state militias, the US Army, and privately financed, armed strikebreakers.

As the economic system engendered one economic crisis after another (1873, 1893, 1901, 1907, 1920, and 1929), immigrants were seen by some residents as taking jobs from those who were already in America – who were, of course, mostly immigrants themselves or descendants of immigrants. Hostility towards newcomers was intensified when the newcomers were Catholics, Jews, or, especially, Asians.

The reaction to Asian immigrants was out of proportion to their number. While tens of *millions* immigrated from Ireland and Germany and later from southern and eastern Europe, only tens of *thousands* came from China and Japan and (in even smaller numbers) from Korea and South Asia.

Some three hundred thousand came from China before immigration from that country was all but ended by the Chinese Exclusion Act of 1882 (noted earlier). Most of those who had come returned to China, leaving a hundred thousand settlers, almost all male. Intermarriage and procreation were limited, and each census revealed that the number of Chinese Americans steadily decreased.

The growth of American industry led to a greatly expanded urban population who were unable to produce their own food. Food became available to cities throughout the continent because immigrants constructed a national railroad network which now acquired refrigerated railroad cars. Chinese workers had helped develop agriculture in the American West as well as the railroads. When Chinese immigrants were barred by law, employers sought new sources of labor, especially for agriculture in the American West.

American interventions abroad opened new sources of labor in the Far East – first in Japan, from which workers began to emigrate. This marked a major change in official Japanese policy. For two centuries Japan, fearing foreign domination, had limited its relations with other countries. Japan's revision of that policy was, however, not entirely voluntary. In 1853 an American fleet entered Edo (later Tokyo) harbor, where Admiral Perry delivered a letter from President Fillmore to the Emperor. When Perry returned the following year with an even larger naval force, Japan agreed, in the Convention of Kanagawa, to open ports to US trade. That agreement was the first of a series of "unequal treaties" (somewhat like the agreements that were then being imposed on China by European powers and the US). The resulting political crises within Japan led to its relaxing emigration restrictions.

Between 1885 and 1924 one hundred and eighty thousand Japanese men and women immigrated to the continental US. (Even more went to Hawai'i, which we will turn to later.) The Japanese newcomers faced conditions like those that had been experienced by their Chinese predecessors. Anti-Asian organizations protested their presence and campaigned for their exclusion. For a while, Japanese immigrants fared somewhat better than the Chinese had. Until the 1906 San Francisco earthquake, for example, the Japanese in that city were not subjected to segregation. Afterwards, however, segregation was imposed, over their vigorous protests. A diplomatic crisis ensued and President Teddy Roosevelt tried but failed to persuade San Francisco to end segregation. The crisis was resolved by a 1907 "Gentlemen's Agreement" between the two governments which committed Japan to end emigration to America.

Many Japanese settled in the West and also contributed greatly to the development of its agriculture. But their rights were limited. In 1878 a federal court had held in the *Ah Yup* case that Chinese Americans were non-white and therefore ineligible for naturalization. The same doctrine was extended to Japanese Americans by the 1922 *Ozawa* case. These rulings ensured the discriminatory application of "alien land laws" that were enacted by the Pacific Coast states starting in 1913. Designed to exclude Japanese Americans from farming, these laws avoided explicit reference to Japanese Americans or any other ethnic group. They said that persons who are "ineligible for citizenship" were prohibited from owning and even leasing farmland. Consistent with its decisions about "color-blind" Jim Crow laws in the South, the Supreme Court in the 1923 case of *Terrace v. Thompson* upheld a Washington state law that banned the leasing of farm land by persons ineligible for citizenship, and the decision was quickly extended to a number of such restrictions.

The pattern of judicial decisions reveals the malleability of the color line. In the 1915 *Dow* case, a federal Circuit Court had ruled that Syrians, who were classified as Caucasian by anthropologists, were eligible for US citizenship. The Court held that, when Congress in 1790 restricted naturalization to white persons, it had been concerned mainly to exclude persons of African ancestry and did not have such groups as Syrians in mind. It said that Congress was presumably aware that courts had been naturalizing Syrians like Dow and inferred that Dow's naturalization was compatible with congressional intentions.

In the 1922 *Ozawa* case, the Supreme Court, supposedly applying the same criterion of whiteness, ruled that Japanese Americans were "clearly" not white and thus were ineligible for citizenship. The following year, however, the Court changed its approach when ruling on the eligibility of the South Asian Bhagat Singh Thind. According to anthropological criteria, Thind was *Caucasian*. The Court said, however, that this dark-skinned person would not be considered *white* by lay persons. For that reason, the Court rejected anthropological guidance and ruled that Thind and other dark-skinned persons were ineligible for citizenship.

In deciding that Asians were ineligible for citizenship, the Court may have been guided by the fact that Congress in 1875 had rejected a Radical Republican proposal to remove all racial restrictions on naturalization, which would have extended eligibility to Asians.

After *Terrace v. Thompson* many Japanese Americans were able to continue farming by assigning ownership of their farms to their American-born children or to helpful white neighbors. But many European Americans in the region resented their presence, and those attitudes found further expression during World War II, when the federal government interned more than one hundred thousand persons of Japanese ancestry, most of whom were American citizens. They were confined in remote "war relocation camps," where US soldiers manning the watchtowers aimed their weapons inside the high fences, at the internees, and occasionally fired upon those who they thought were trying to escape, killing some. During their internment, many families lost most of their possessions. Some lost hope and suffered acute depression.

The internment program survived judicial review, although it applied only to Japanese Americans and not to German Americans or Italian Americans, whose ethnic homelands were equally at war with the US. In the 1943 *Hirabayashi* case, the Supreme Court upheld a curfew order against Japanese Americans in the Pacific coastal region, supposedly to prevent sabotage and espionage. The Court then applied that precedent in the 1944 *Korematsu* case, which upheld an order excluding Japanese Americans from those districts. Justice Black, observing that such restrictions required "strict scrutiny" to determine their constitutionality, held that they were not racist.

When the case was reopened in 1984, Korematsu's conviction was set aside on the ground that the federal government had withheld relevant information from the Court in 1944. Government lawyers had defended the internment orders as if the federal security and intelligence services agreed with General DeWitt, the West Coast military commander, who claimed that the internment of Japanese Americans was needed to prevent sabotage and espionage. A review in the early 1980s of government records revealed, however, that all the federal security and intelligence agencies had disagreed with General DeWitt. In 1984 embarrassed government lawyers declined to defend the internment policies, and Korematsu's conviction was set aside.

Two considerations suggest that in the 1940s the government had behaved even worse than the 1984 ruling acknowledged. In the first place, the Supreme Court had before it strong evidence that the government's justification for the internment of Japanese Americans should not have survived strict scrutiny: the racist character of General DeWitt's arguments, which was noted by the dissenting justices. Justice Murphy identified fatal infirmities of the government's case and observed that its internment procedures had left ample time for individualized hearings, and thus due process, which the government had declined to employ, although allies of America such as Great Britain had done so and the US had also done so for persons of German or Italian ancestry.

Secondly, no mass internment of Japanese Americans occurred during World War II in Hawai'i, despite the fact that Japanese Americans in Hawai'i comprised a larger group than those on America's Pacific coast as well as a much greater percentage of the local population, and that Hawai'i – far out in the Pacific Ocean, much closer to Japan and one of the principal targets of Japan's attack in December, 1941 – was in a much more vulnerable position than the American West Coast. General Emmons, the military commander on Hawai'i, regarded the mass internment orders as unjustifiable, protested to Washington, and refused to implement them. In this he was supported by business, labor, and the media in Hawai'i, which contrasted sharply with the situation on the West Coast. General Emmons observed that the mass internment of Japanese Americans on Hawai'i would cripple its economy and undermine the wartime mobilization. As a result, only 1% of the islands' one hundred and forty thousand Japanese Americans was interned.

To return to our narrative: immigration from most of Asia was ended by the Asiatic Barred Zone Act of 1917, after which many immigrants came from Mexico and the Philippine Islands (which the US had acquired in its 1898 war with Spain). Mexico has always been an especially convenient source of labor for American employers, because travel and entry obstacles were minimal and nativistic objections to Mexicans' presence could be addressed by mass deportations – as was done during the Great Depression of the 1930s.

The total number of immigrants from Asia – a few hundred thousand – was actually quite small from a national perspective. Vastly greater numbers of immigrants (many millions) arrived from Europe during the decades prior to World War I. Their presence also had profound effects on US policies.

During the twenty-five year period between 1890 and 1915, the US population increased by thirty-five million, nearly half of which stemmed from immigration. But the reaction to these immigrants reflected more than their sheer numbers. Almost all came from southern or eastern Europe or Russia, many were Catholics or Jews, and their presence activated ancient hatreds.

Americans' negative reactions to such immigration led rapidly to unprecedented restrictions on immigration from Europe. In 1921 Congress enacted the Emergency Quota Act, which limited the number of immigrants from a given country in a year to 3% of the number of US residents from that country according to the census of 1910. That measure was soon regarded as too hospitable, and the National Origins Act of 1924 reduced the national quotas per year to *2%* of the number of US residents from a given country according to the *1890* census. This formula ensured that the quotas would not be enlarged by the fifteen million or so newcomers who had arrived between 1890 and 1910, and it all but closed the door to further immigration from southern and eastern Europe, including Russia. The 1924 act also continued the ban on immigration from the "Asian-Pacific Triangle," and it regulated immigration to America for the next forty-one years.

But those laws did not limit immigration from other nations of the Americas. Mexico and Puerto Rico would soon become America's principal sources of readily accessible – and disposable – labor.

The groups most affected by the immigration restrictions that were imposed between 1882 and 1924 – Asians, Catholics, and Jews – had racial credentials that were suspect to American nativists. The American eugenics movement (which was most influential during this period) agitated for racial purification through measures such as sterilization, which were implemented by some American states and approved by federal courts.

The American eugenics movement's doctrines influenced those of the Third Reich, which applied them with ruthless efficiency a short time later, especially in places known as Auschwitz, Chelmno, Belzec, Majdanek, Sobibor, and Treblinka.

14

AN AMERICAN EMPIRE

Before 1898 the US lacked overseas colonies. With the exception of Alaska (purchased from Russia in 1867), all of America's previous accessions bordered its territory, were viewed as areas for settlement by European Americans, and evolved into states of the Union. After 1898, however, none of that could be assumed of American territorial acquisitions. The US acquired distant nations whose peoples were not regarded by Americans as white, which were not seen as areas for white settlement and were not expected to become states of the Union. They were desired as markets, for their resources, as sources of labor supply, and for military purposes. More than a century later, one of them has achieved statehood, but only after sixty-three years.

The new American possessions included the Hawaiian Islands, situated more than two thousand miles from the America mainland, and some of Spain's few remaining colonies, most notably Puerto Rico and the Philippines, the latter more than seven thousand miles away. When the US took possession of those nations, Cuba broke free of Spain; but under the coercive presence of American troops Cuba was unable to achieve its long-sought independence and became instead an American protectorate.

In 1903, with US military support, Panama seceded from Colombia and America acquired sovereignty over the Canal Zone, which, upon completion of the Panama Canal in 1914, gave the US control of the best shipping route between the Atlantic and Pacific Oceans. America was also busy developing financial, industrial, and military control of Central America and the West Indies. America had created an overseas empire.

Let's begin with Hawai'i. When a British fleet under Captain James Cook came upon the islands in the late eighteenth century, Hawaiians had a diversified agriculture, abundant seafood, woven cloth that would be widely admired, and enviable navigation skills. They bartered goods but not land.

Sailors and naval officers found the islands a convenient place to secure supplies and sexual diversion on voyages between the Americas and the Far East. They discovered some of the islands' resources, such as sandalwood, which they then harvested and exported until there was little left. They introduced buying and selling for profit as well as alcohol and prostitution.

The islands' population of four or five hundred thousand lacked immunity to diseases that were communicated by visiting sailors, and within half a century its native population was reduced to a hundred thousand.

Early in the nineteenth century American missionaries arrived. They campaigned against alcohol and prostitution and developed schools, a Hawaiian alphabet, and printing. Some Americans became Hawaiian citizens; some married into Hawaiian families and gained influence. The islands had been unified under a king, who the Americans persuaded to change the land tenure system. The king then allocated most of the land to the kingdom and the chiefs, including himself, leaving just thirty thousand acres out of forty million for the use of ordinary Hawaiians.

Appreciating Hawai'i's strategic position and splendid harbor, several European nations sought possession of the islands. They secured land rights and commerce, but the new American elite helped the king negotiate treaties that promised Hawai'i's continued independence.

In 1835 Americans secured the first long-term land lease for a sugar plantation. Sugar production developed rapidly, and accelerated after 1875 when Hawai'i and the US agreed to a Treaty of Reciprocity that allowed Hawaiian sugar to enter the US free of import duties. This reduced the net price of Hawaiian sugar in the US and gave American sugar planters in Hawai'i a virtual monopoly in the American market. Hawai'i's sugar production increased from ninety-four hundred tons in 1870 to three hundred thousand tons in 1900. Sugar became Hawai'i's chief export and the principal segment of its economy, which was now controlled by American expatriates.

Sugar production requires land and labor. Land became available for purchase because of changes the Americans had promoted in the land tenure system. But labor had to be imported, for by then the indigenous population was not large and in any case Hawaiians preferred independent farming and fishing to laboring on plantations. So the planters recruited workers from abroad: forty-six thousand from China, two hundred thousand from Japan, one hundred and ten thousand from the Philippines, and a few thousand from Korea and South Asia. Before long Asians comprised a large majority of Hawai'i's population.

The American elite on Hawai'i sought its annexation by the United States. But their increasing domination of the islands, combined with their attitudes towards Native Hawaiians (which were condescending at best), created resentment and resistance. So the Americans took steps to ensure control. In 1887 members of the missionary and business community forced the king to accept new political arrangements. The resulting "Bayonet Constitution" enabled non-Hawaiian white residents to dominate the Hawaiian government. In 1893 the US Minister to Hawai'i called in American marines to help American missionaries and business leaders overthrow the monarchy altogether. The Americans forced the queen to abdicate and established a Provisional Government which disfranchised most Hawaiians. The US annexed the formerly independent kingdom during the Spanish–American War, when Hawai'i was seen as a useful coaling station for the US Navy, which had assumed a global role.

The 1898 war with Spain was ignited in the Caribbean. It remains unclear who caused the destruction of the USS *Maine* in Havana harbor, which was the rationale for an American declaration of war. Spain was not prepared to fight a war against the US, for at the time it was failing to put down armed independence movements in Cuba and the Philippines. Philippine rebels had gained control of almost all of their archipelago, except for the city of Manila, and Cuban rebels had very nearly overcome Spanish military resistance.

Reports of Spain's repressive policies in Cuba had generated American sympathy for the rebel cause, which led Congress to append the Teller Amendment to its war resolution, pledging *not* to annex Cuba. After American forces invaded the island, however, the American military commander excluded Cuban rebels from negotiations with the colonial government and kept colonial officials in office after the Spanish surrender. The rebels established an independent government, but the US continued its military occupation of the island until the Cuban constitutional convention agreed to the Platt Amendment, which gave America control over Cuban foreign and domestic policy and the right to intervene as America saw fit. The Teller Amendment was respected in form only.

Such uses of American military force abroad were not in fact a departure from established practice. Prior to the war with Spain, the US had employed troops and warships scores of times for the purpose of protecting American interests in Argentina, Brazil, Colombia, Haiti, Nicaragua, Paraguay, Peru, and Uruguay. That policy continued. Between the war with Spain and World War II the US military occupied Cuba (from 1898 to 1902 and from 1917 to 1922), the Dominican Republic (1916–24), Haiti (1915–34) and Nicaragua (1912–25 and 1926–33). Military occupations became less frequent after World War II, replaced largely by covert US operations, as in Guatemala, Cuba, Brazil, Chile, Argentina, Nicaragua, El Salvador, Venezuela, and Haiti.

American investments were substantial throughout Latin America, many of the region's resources were owned by American corporations, and a number of Latin American nations had substantial debts to American banks. This enabled American creditors to control national policies of those countries and secure additional economic advantages. The de facto American empire encompassed much of the Western hemisphere.

Unlike other nations of the Americas that were dominated by American interests, Puerto Rico was an official colony. Its formal relations to the US were regulated by the Foraker Act of 1900 which provided for a governor appointed by the US President and a legislature with limited authority, its enactments subject to a US veto. Puerto Ricans became American "nationals," a status short of citizenship which allowed them to travel freely to and reside in the United States.

Puerto Ricans became increasingly frustrated by their subordination and agitated for independence. Congress responded in 1917 by conferring American citizenship on the islanders. In 1948 – fifty years after the US acquired the island from Spain – Puerto Ricans were permitted to elect their own governor, and in 1952 the island acquired "commonwealth" status, which involved somewhat greater autonomy, but no representation in the US Congress. And so it remains to this day.

The Philippine conflict was much longer and much bloodier than America's war against Spain in the Caribbean. Like the Cubans, the Philippine rebels were excluded by the US military from negotiations regarding the Spanish surrender, and they were excluded entirely from Manila. War ensued between the US and Philippine independence forces, which resulted in US casualties in the thousands and Filipino losses in the hundreds of thousands, many of them non-combatants. Although the US declared in 1902 that the war was over, guerilla warfare continued for another decade. That was possible because independence forces received wide popular support. As in the war it would later conduct in Vietnam, the US military understood that its enemy was not simply an army but the population at large – which helps to explain the American willingness to wipe out entire Filipino communities and the scale of non-combatant Filipino casualties. Such is the price of empire.

Like Puerto Ricans, Filipinos did not become American citizens but were classified as US "nationals." That allowed them to migrate to Hawai'i and the American mainland without restriction and enabled American employers to recruit them in large numbers.

Filipinos were subjected, however, to racist maltreatment and resentment, which came to a head during the Great Depression. The Tydings-McDuffie Act of 1934 promised the Philippines independence within ten years, but also declared Filipinos aliens in the US, so that they could no longer move freely to the mainland. The promise of independence was kept, though its fulfillment was delayed until 1946 by World War II. And the US has maintained military bases in the Philippine archipelago, to the consternation of many Filipinos.

15

THE GREAT MIGRATION

The establishment of Jim Crow was doubly dispiriting to black Southerners, especially those who had survived slavery and experienced Reconstruction. After a promising period of relative freedom they were subjected once again to conditions that resembled slavery. Few African Americans had been able to achieve and retain economic independence, all lost civil rights, all faced unpredictable brutality, and they lacked legal recourse for such wrongs.

Many sharecroppers were cheated by plantation owners' accounting methods, but to complain of being cheated by a white planter would be fruitless and indeed dangerous. Those who were cheated but not immobilized by indebtedness would seek better arrangements elsewhere. As a consequence, many sharecroppers moved every two or three years, seeking better conditions. But vacancies were rare at plantations with honest owners, for their sharecroppers would have less reason to leave.

The psychological and intellectual cost to African Americans of living under Jim Crow was terrible. For their personal safety black children had to learn to defer to white individuals of all ages and conditions and to suppress reasonable outrage at indignities and mistreatment. Educational opportunities were limited. Inadequate support for black schools guaranteed poor facilities and might also result in a shortened school year. Children of agricultural workers were often needed to help their families in the fields, especially during harvest season.

Non-agricultural work was severely limited. Black women might become domestic servants. Black teachers could work only in black schools, were paid significantly less than their white counterparts, and then only for that portion of the year that their schools were open. Some African Americans managed to become physicians, but their practices were limited to the black community. Few hospitals served black patients, which severely limited the medical resources that were available to black doctors and the medical care that was available to black patients. All of these conditions continued well past World War II.

Black Southerners thus had good reason to leave if something better was accessible. The North promised freedom and employment in the periods surrounding the two world wars, when military mobilization led to hiring for some existing jobs and some that were newly created. American industry expanded rapidly, especially manufacturing, steel, meat packing and railroads, while immigration was stopped from Asia and was reduced greatly from Europe by war and the new restrictions. Northern employers looked south and saw potential employees who could be paid less than white workers but who could nonetheless be attracted by the prospect of higher wages than they could receive in the South. So Northern employers sent labor recruiters south, to be rewarded according to the number of workers for whom they could be credited.

Potential migrants also learned of job opportunities from Northern black communities, through newspapers such as the *Chicago Defender*, and from relatives, friends, and acquaintances who had already migrated.

The emigration of black Southerners was resisted by planters through threats, interceptions, and attacks on recruiters. Sometimes migrants had to steal away by night. In the 1940s some planters' attitudes were changed by development of the mechanized cotton picker, which could do the work of fifty humans. This reduced the need for labor on cotton plantations and gave more black Southerners reason to seek work elsewhere.

As a consequence, four hundred and fifty thousand African Americans left the South in the 1910s and eight hundred thousand did so during the 1920s. The migration slowed during the 1930s, when jobs were scarce throughout the country, but even then another four hundred thousand left the South. With the mobilization for World War II, a million and a half African Americans migrated north or west during the 1940s. Another million or million and a half moved from the South during the 1950s, and between eight hundred thousand and one million four hundred thousand migrated in the 1960s.

The routes they took and their destinations were determined by the available means of transportation, mainly the existing rail lines. African Americans from Florida, Georgia, and South Carolina traveled to the District of Columbia, Newark, or New York City. From Louisiana, Mississippi, and Alabama they went to Chicago, Milwaukee, or Detroit. Some traveled by car from Texas, Oklahoma, and Louisiana to San Diego, Los Angeles, or Oakland.

In the earlier decades of this Great Migration, black workers might be recruited as strike breakers, which put them at odds with white workers whose unions were likely to have excluded people of color. But conditions would improve with the rise of industrial unions in the 1930s.

New migrants were aided by African Americans who had arrived earlier, but the transition could be difficult. Northern city ways were unfamiliar, the cost of living was higher than down South, and a family in the city was unlikely to have a garden for essential foods. And in the North African Americans were still subject to lower wages and exclusion from many job categories.

African Americans were not generally welcomed in Northern cities, and their hostile reception helped to create the residential segregation that persists today. Rapid urbanization led to an increasing demand for housing that could not fully be satisfied, especially when workers and construction materials were diverted to military uses. This led to housing shortages felt most severely by the least affluent communities.

Most immigrants from abroad from the mid-nineteenth to the mid-twentieth centuries could afford only the cheapest housing and gravitated to communities with people of like origin. Ethnic enclaves developed of Chinese, Germans, Greeks, Japanese, Irish, Italians, Poles, and eastern European Jews. But none of those groups experienced the concentration of ethnicity or the extent and persistence of geographical isolation that would be experienced by African Americans. By 1940 the isolation of black residents within Northern cities was greater than had ever been experienced by any other ethnic group in America, and the condition was not temporary. European newcomers resided initially in communities of immigrants that were ethnically heterogeneous, most lived outside such enclaves, and such concentrations as existed were temporary. Not so for African Americans.

Development of the black urban "ghetto" resulted in part from exclusionary actions by private parties, such as homeowners, real estate agents, and providers of home mortgage loans and insurance. The means used included restrictive covenants, which prohibited the sale of particular properties to black families and perhaps members of other disfavored groups; white boycotts of real estate agents who served black clients; the systematic diversion by real estate agents of black clients from white communities; bombs directed at homes in white residential neighborhoods into which African Americans had moved; and "block-busting," whereby African Americans are brought into a previously all-white neighborhood as property owners or renters, leading the least tolerant white families to leave, making room for more black families to move in, leading less intolerant white families to leave, and so on, while black families acquired housing at inflated rents and prices. "Redlining" identified black neighborhoods on loan officers' maps to show where home purchase and home improvement loans were to be denied or interest rates inflated. This practice increased the difficulty and cost of a black family's acquiring and maintaining a home.

Public policies also contributed. Racially restrictive zoning was initially employed, until it was ruled unconstitutional in 1917. The Federal Housing Administration endorsed redlining in the 1930s. After World War II, governments constructed new highways to serve white suburbs but withheld construction of public transportation that would enable black workers to commute from suburbs at lower cost. Public housing authorities enforced racial segregation in their facilities, and when they were ordered by courts to stop the practice, funding for public housing disappeared.

"White flight" from racially heterogeneous cities to white suburbs is possible only when those suburbs are kept exclusively white. This requires the cooperation of real estate agents and local governments whose zoning practices discourage or prevent low income housing, e.g., by mandating large lot sizes for new houses or prohibiting multi-unit housing construction.

When housing discrimination was prohibited by law, real estate agents developed covert measures to divert black renters and home buyers away from white communities. Such practices can be identified by "audits" in which, for example, two sets of prospective clients would visit real estate or rental agents. The first couple would be identifiable as black, the second, immediately following, would be identifiable as white. The two couples would have otherwise similar social profiles, including the ability to pay. Discriminatory practices would be revealed when the white couple was provided with housing options not offered to the immediately preceding black couple.

Non-governmental organizations conducted housing audits, especially under the Comprehensive Employment and Training Act of 1973, which supported a variety of anti-poverty jobs in non-profit organizations. CETA was replaced by the Job Training Partnership Act of 1982 which did not support such programs.

Congress enacted a Fair Housing Act in 1968, but only after it was stripped of enforcement provisions. When enforcement was provided by the Fair Housing Amendment Act of 1988, the federal government declined to enforce fair housing rules vigorously. Congress enacted the Housing and Community Development Act of 1974, the Home Mortgage Disclosure Act of 1975, and the Community Reinvestment Act of 1977, but inadequate resources were devoted to their weak enforcement provisions, and there was resistance from real estate agents and local politicians, with the result that the anti-discrimination provisions of those measures have had minimal effect.

Thus, public policies and private practices created the black urban ghetto and have since cooperated to maintain residential segregation.

16

SURVIVING AND DEFYING JIM CROW

Jim Crow was entrenched during a period filled with racist messages, such as the 1915 film *Birth of a Nation* which depicted African Americans as unsuited for political office and black men as sexually aggressive. It depicted the Ku Klux Klan as a necessary means of rescuing the South from ill-conceived Reconstruction policies.

Black critics protested showings of the film and sought to counter its message with a widespread educational campaign. The film appears, however, to have sparked racist pogroms in American cities and to have helped revive the Klan.

Organizations like the Klan were but one control mechanism of Jim Crow. Such a system can be maintained only with the constant threat of severe penalties for insubordination or resistance. Black women, men, and children were expected to accept inferior incomes, jobs, and living conditions as well as unpredictable humiliations and unwarranted attacks by whites – as described, for example, in Richard's Wright's memoir of growing up black in the South, *The Ethics of Living Jim Crow*.

African Americans developed what W.E.B. Du Bois called a "double consciousness," viewing oneself from a biased white perspective while recognizing one's own true value, a facility that white members of society did not need to acquire. Internalizing that contradiction adds to the debilitating stresses of navigating Jim Crow. How could one possibly survive?

Some were not permitted to survive. We do not know what triggered many of the lynchings to which African Americans were subjected but we do know that "uppity" men and women who resisted outrageous treatment or the burdens of unrelenting subordination were favored targets of brutal retribution.

Those who survived included a diverse group of outstanding individuals who related to Jim Crow in a variety of ways. Some African Americans advocated acceptance of subordination. That was Booker T. Washington's apparent message when he addressed the Atlanta Exposition of 1895. Born a slave, in 1881 Washington founded the Tuskegee Institute, which was dedicated to preparing young African Americans for a life of physical labor or domestic service. His "Atlanta Compromise" address promised the white audience "that you and your families will be surrounded by the most patient, faithful, law-abiding and unresentful people that the world has seen." Given this public position, Washington's projects, which included the development of schools for African Americans throughout the South, attracted wealthy and powerful supporters. Washington became the most influential African American of his time, whose advice was sought by the first President Roosevelt, among many others.

It is unclear that Washington meant exactly what he seemed to say in Atlanta, for he quietly supported legal challenges to segregation and disfranchisement. He appears to have believed that public agitation for civil rights would be counter-productive in the circumstances, and to have regarded accommodation as the only policy with a chance of securing equality in the long run.

Ida B. Wells-Barnett, a contemporary of Washington's, who was also born under slavery, did not accept either his counsel of quietude or the retiring role that was conventionally assigned to women. A teacher, journalist, and tireless political organizer, she campaigned for many years against lynching and for women's rights. Seemingly fearless, she advocated armed self-defense by African Americans. Her most famous writings include *Southern Horrors* and *A Red Record*, which discredited Southern excuses for lynchings.

Du Bois, the pre-eminent black scholar, publicly disagreed with Washington. In *The Souls of Black Folk*, he argued that African Americans should not accept consignment to lives of physical labor or domestic service, that advanced education should be available to African Americans who can best use it, and that black men and women must struggle for civil rights through political organization and legal initiatives. In 1909 Du Bois, Wells-Barnett, and others founded the National Association for the Advancement of Colored People (NAACP). Du Bois went on to edit its publication, *The Crisis*, for many years. He was a consistently radical and public critic of the color line.

Another recipient of Du Bois' criticism was his contemporary Marcus Garvey, who believed that white Americans would never regard black Americans as equals. Instead of fruitless striving for civil rights in America, he advocated emigration to Africa. A charismatic figure, during the 1920s Garvey achieved an exceptionally wide following in the black community. Perhaps for that reason, Garvey worried officials who were committed to the status quo, such as J. Edgar Hoover, head of the US Justice Department's Bureau of Investigation. Garvey was prosecuted for mail fraud, served time in prison, and was then deported to his native Jamaica.

While Garvey's organization was flourishing, A. Philip Randolph was organizing the Brotherhood of Sleeping Car Porters, one of the most effective organizations for black workers and a leading force within the black community.

The previous century's Knights of Labor had recruited African Americans into trade unions and the twentieth century's Industrial Workers of the World brought black and white workers together into a more fully unified organization, but they were exceptions to prevailing labor union practices. Unions had a mixed record of admitting African Americans and addressing their exclusion from job opportunities, especially in the skilled trades, which dominated the American Federation of Labor. Encroachments on the color line varied greatly by industry, union leadership, employers' reactions, and local conditions. As the railroad sleeping car porters were predominantly black and the 1920s were a period of intensified racism and discrimination, Randolph's project made good sense.

Randolph never limited his organizing efforts to union work. Committed to socialism and racial equality, he opposed American involvement in World War I. Twenty years later, as World War II was beginning, America's production of war material rapidly increased, along with the number of industrial jobs. Randolph and others organized a 1941 march on Washington to end racial discrimination in war industries and the US military. This persuaded President Franklin Roosevelt to issue an executive order establishing a Fair Employment Practices Committee to monitor employment under government contracts. In response, the march was called off. The second aim of the planned march was achieved in 1948 when Roosevelt's successor, Harry Truman, issued an executive order ending racial segregation in America's armed forces. In 1963 Randolph helped organize the march on Washington that did come off – the one that is known for Martin Luther King, Jr.'s "I Have a Dream" speech.

Randolph's career spanned many crucial developments of the twentieth century. These included President Wilson's re-segregation of federal offices, the Harlem Renaissance, the *Scottsboro* case, the Great Depression, and the New Deal. The latter four merit more attention.

The Harlem Renaissance was an intense flowering of African American arts and letters in New York City, especially during the 1920s and 1930s. The Great Migration of black Southerners gave rise to a number of large multi-class black communities in the North and West. As New York became the cultural center of America, Harlem became a center of black culture. African American arts and letters had begun to emerge two centuries earlier but leapt forward between World War I and the Great Depression. Distinctive, innovative, and influential black music was composed and performed; in the case of jazz, it was often created while it was being performed. Poetry, novels, short stories, plays, the visual arts, and non-fiction writing (often political) arose within an expanding creative community. A very short list of individuals who are associated with the Harlem Renaissance would include Romaire Bearden, Countee Cullen, Duke Ellington, Billie Holliday, Langston Hughes, Zora Neale Hurston, James Weldon Johnson, Jacob Lawrence, Paul Robeson, and Richard Wright.

The *Scottsboro* case began in 1931 with a false accusation and the arrest for rape of nine black teenage boys in Alabama, who were subjected to a set of grossly unfair trials. If not for outside support and legal assistance (in this case from the American Communist Party), eight of the boys would have been executed in accordance with the death sentences they received. The convictions were appealed once in vain to the Alabama Supreme Court and twice successfully to the US Supreme Court. The latter sent the cases back for retrial because African Americans had systematically been excluded from jury service – a landmark ruling, as it recognized as unconstitutional a discriminatory social practice that was not required by Jim Crow law. Despite repeated convictions under biased conditions, none of the boys were ultimately executed. That alone was an unusual accomplishment.

The Great Depression of the 1930s brought extremely high unemployment, a great many farm bankruptcies, and widespread privation, especially to the many millions on the economic margins, in which people of color were disproportionately represented. In 1933 it also brought Franklin Roosevelt to the American presidency, and his "New Deal." At Roosevelt's urging, a Democratic-controlled Congress began to develop programs to address urgent needs, such as creating jobs. As a result of the differences between Roosevelt's reform program and his Republican predecessor's economic inactivity, in 1936 many African Americans abandoned the Republican Party and voted for the Democratic Party, which Roosevelt represented.

But the Democrats' majority in Congress depended on representatives from the Jim Crow South, and the New Deal's promise far exceeded its actual benefits for people of color. Many of the new federal programs discriminated against Americans of color or excluded them entirely.

To take a few examples: the Federal Housing Administration would not guarantee mortgage loans for black families who wished to move into white neighborhoods. The Civilian Conservation Corps, which provided jobs under federal construction projects, maintained racially segregated camps for workers. The Agricultural Adjustment Act required that farm acreage be reduced in order to lower output and raise prices; this helped farmers who could afford to reduce the acreage they committed to crops, but it caused more than a hundred thousand African Americans to lose their farms and ignored the needs of sharecroppers and tenant farmers. Unemployment insurance and old-age pensions under the Social Security Act excluded agricultural and domestic workers, which effectively left out most black Southerners. The same was true of the National Labor Relations Act, which eliminated barriers to collective bargaining and effective unionization, and the Fair Labor Standards Act, which established minimum wages and maximum hours for employees – neither covered sharecroppers or domestic workers.

African Americans benefitted under some New Deal programs, such as the Works Progress Administration, which provided work relief, built many Southern schools and hospitals, and allocated funds without racial bias. By enabling unionization, the National Labor Relations Act allowed black workers to gain from the enhanced bargaining power of the rising industrial unions, which were more welcoming to African Americans than older trade unions. The Farm Security

Administration provided camps for migratory farm workers, which included many desperate white and black farmers who had lost their land.

As it happened, Native Americans benefitted more consistently than other impoverished groups from New Deal reforms during the Great Depression. In 1928 a study of federal Indian policy known as the Meriam Report concluded that the allotment system under the General Allotment (Dawes) Act of 1887 had been disastrous for Indians. A skeptical US Senate conducted its own study, which came to the same conclusion in the early 1930s. This led to the Indian Reorganization Act of 1934, which ended the allotment program. Perhaps because the continued existence of Indian tribes and Native Americans posed no apparent threat to European American territorial settlement and their exploitation of the natural resources of Native American territory, the government suspended its efforts at terminating tribes, stopped trying to eliminate indigenous languages and culture, and provided funds for land purchases, schools, hospitals, and local agencies with programs that aided Native Americans. These policy reforms presumably contributed to the gradual, steady increase in the Native American population that had been underway since the turn of the century.

Other Americans of color did not fare well under the New Deal. As we have noted, hundreds of thousands of Mexican Americans, including many US citizens, were deported during the Great Depression. And most Japanese Americans would be placed in concentration camps during World War II.

Conditions would change considerably with the rise of the Civil Rights Movement after World War II, during the Cold War. The Movement would be developed in part by relatively new organizations, such as the Congress of Racial Equality (CORE), founded in 1942, as well as organizations that would soon arise. That story continues below.

17

THE SECOND RECONSTRUCTION

During the Reconstruction of 1865 to 1877, Congress challenged the color line by enacting laws and proposing constitutional amendments, which were quickly ratified, that ended slavery and sought a significant degree of racial equality. As we have seen, these measures faced presidential opposition and were undermined by judicial hostility and violent resistance. When the former slaves were unable to achieve economic independence, had recourse to tenant farming and share-cropping, and then were subjected to the convict leasing system, abolition was in many respects undone. Unreconstructed white supremacists regained control of the former slave states and, with no federal opposition, created the system called Jim Crow.

World War II generated the conditions for another major challenge to the color line. The two decades of civil rights reform that followed have been labeled the "Second Reconstruction," and the term seems apt, as egalitarian changes were once again made in the law and the reforms once again were met with violent resistance and a backlash that reversed substantial gains. We'll first review the government's role and then consider the Civil Rights Movement itself.

The Second Reconstruction developed differently from the first, for this time all three branches of the federal government contributed. Harry Truman became president in 1945 upon the death of Franklin Roosevelt, just as Andrew Johnson did in 1865, following Lincoln's assassination. But Truman did not follow Andrew Johnson's example. In 1946 Truman formed a committee to study the condition of civil rights in America and make recommendations for improvement. In 1948, a few months after receiving the committee's report, Truman ordered that the armed forces be desegregated. In successfully seeking his party's nomination for the presidency that same year, Truman embraced a civil rights platform that he knew would lose him support from Southern Democrats, who indeed left the Democratic Party and formed a competing States' Rights (or "Dixiecrat") party.

After World War II, the Supreme Court did not follow the example set by the Court following the Civil War: it did not undermine legislation and executive orders that challenged the color line. Instead, it supported reform, most notably by ruling in its 1954 *Brown v. Board of Education* decision that racial segregation in public schools was unconstitutional. The Court went on to uphold subsequent civil rights legislation and its enforcement.

This time Congress, which included influential representatives of the Jim Crow South, was slower than the other federal branches to challenge the color line. Its civil rights acts of 1957 and 1960 were weak and ineffective. But much had changed by 1964 when Congress, though seriously divided, enacted a strong and enforceable Civil Rights Act, which outlawed the color line and other kinds of discrimination in schools, jobs, and public accommodations. A year later Congress enacted the Voting Rights Act, which created effective means of ending discriminatory electoral practices.

So civil rights legislation was enacted, it was judicially sustained, and it was enforced. The color line was officially condemned and white supremacist rhetoric became unacceptable in the public sphere. As had happened a century earlier, however, the color line was defended vigorously and violently and a backlash followed; but more on that later.

Crucial aspects of the Second Reconstruction could not have been predicted. For example, no one expected Truman to promote civil rights. He was just a politician from the border state of Missouri who had been chosen for political reasons to be Franklin Roosevelt's running mate in 1944, replacing the more progressive Henry Wallace.

Much the same applies to Lyndon Johnson of Texas. While majority leader of the Senate, he had worked with other Southern senators to strip the 1957 and 1960 civil rights bills of their capacity to enforce civil rights. As president following John Kennedy's assassination, however, Johnson not only signed into law the decidedly more significant civil rights enactments of 1964 and 1965, but also campaigned vigorously for their passage.

As a body, the post-war Congress could not have been expected to contribute much to civil rights. Many of its committees were chaired by Southern Democrats and several committees were active promoters of the post-war Red Scare, which linked support for civil rights with subversion and disloyalty. Its civil rights enactments of 1957 and 1960 were empty gestures, incapable of weakening the color line. In 1964 and 1965, however, Congress enacted two of America's most effective civil rights laws.

The Supreme Court had been ruling against aspects of Jim Crow, such as white primaries (*Smith v. Allwright* 1944), segregation in interstate transportation (*Morgan v. Virginia* 1946), racially restrictive covenants (*Shelley v. Kraemer* 1948), and university segregation (*Sweatt v. Painter* and *McLaurin v. Oklahoma* 1950). But those decisions did not suggest that the Court would break with its own long-established precedent and reject the "separate but equal" doctrine. The Court not only did that for public schools in its *Brown* decision, however, but went on to support more expansive civil rights laws.

How to explain the federal government's new position? Let's consider the domestic circumstances first and then turn to the international setting.

Between 1910 and 1950 more than three million African Americans moved from the Jim Crow South to Northern cities, seeking work as well as freedom. New industrial unions rose in the 1930s, first as temporary units within the American Federation of Labor, then under the new Congress of Industrial Organizations. The AFL neglected unskilled workers and its trade unions excluded laborers of color – two groups who, because of Jim Crow practices, greatly overlapped. CIO unions were more inclusive: they gained size and strength by including black workers; as industrial unions they represented both skilled and unskilled workers; and many CIO organizers were left-wingers, including communists, who opposed the color line. So black workers were able to secure not only jobs and union protections but also the chance to enter skilled trades within major industries.

State labor laws had disfavored unions, e.g., by authorizing injunctions against peaceful strikes and treating collective labor actions as violations of anti-trust laws. The Norris-LaGuardia Act of 1932 changed that, but unions were even more firmly legitimated by the National Labor Relations Act of 1935, which authorized collective bargaining and created the National Labor Relations Board to oversee such matters. Despite the Great Depression, union membership increased rapidly in major industries, such as steel and auto manufacturing. And important unions became supporters of social reform.

During World War II many Americans of color volunteered for military service. US forces were segregated, but units comprising African Americans, Native Americans, Asian Americans, or Latinos earned distinguished records in some of the most dangerous and demanding circumstances.

Meanwhile, many African Americans became voters in their new Northern homes, where it was much easier for eligible blacks to register than it was in the Jim Crow South. Following waves of the Great Migration, they voted in numbers large enough to affect the outcomes of elections. Politicians began to view African Americans as a significant voting bloc and adjusted their positions accordingly. Thus, when Truman championed civil rights while seeking the Democratic Party's presidential nomination in 1948, he may well have supposed that he would gain more political support than he would lose. That prediction would have been sound. Despite Southern Democrats' opposition, Truman was elected president. When Johnson later pressed Congress to enact the civil rights bills of 1964 and 1965, he understood that he would lose support in the South, but also that African Americans were abandoning the Republican Party and turning to the Democrats.

Veterans of color returned home from World War II determined to exercise democratic rights for which the war against fascism had supposedly been fought.

During the War America's domestic propaganda stressed racial "tolerance" in opposition to the racist policies of its military opponents, especially Nazi Germany. In the post-war South, however, armed white men blocked black veterans' access to voting registrars and ballot boxes. Regarded as "uppity niggers," black veterans in uniforms with combat medals were assaulted or murdered. Predictably, their killers could not be found or, if found, could not be convicted.

At the same time there was evidence within the wider white community of a willingness to relax the color line. One of the most widely appreciated signs involved a black veteran, Jack Roosevelt (Jackie) Robinson, who had rebelled while in service against the military's color line. An exceptional athlete in several sports, Robinson was recruited by the Brooklyn Dodgers to break the color line in major league baseball. Many players and team owners objected but, with great discipline, Robinson succeeded in 1947. Of course, he had to be better than good: his achievement was only possible because of his outstanding athletic performance.

Now let us relate these domestic developments to international conditions. At the war's end, the world recognized that the Nazi state had conducted a racist Holocaust. Although America had done little to undermine the wartime genocide, after the war the US government supported the recently formed United Nations, which soon endorsed a Universal Declaration of Human Rights. The US and its allies officially supported self-determination for colonized nations (although the US has never applied that principle to Puerto Rico). Decolonization on a wide scale followed, spurred by colonial rebellions. The newly independent, post-colonial nations of color acquired strategic importance, for a "Cold War" had begun between states that were allied with the Soviet Union and those linked with the United States, each bloc vying for influence, raw materials, and markets in the "Third World." America's color line harmed its image and influence abroad. News broadcasts sent film and later televised images around the world, which sometimes showed American police attacking African Americans who were demonstrating peacefully for civil rights. That greatly displeased the designers and administrators of US foreign policy.

The Supreme Court appears to have been influenced by the widespread condemnation of racism and its Cold War significance. The latter point was stressed by the federal government when it supported the challenge by the National Association for the Advancement of Colored People to segregated schools in the *Brown* case.

The Cold War also affected the Second Reconstruction in a contrary way. As we have noted, a central component of the Cold War was a "Red Scare" which treated supporters of liberal reform as domestic enemies. Those who conducted the campaign against "communists" and "fellow travelers" reinforced the color line by regarding sympathy for civil rights as "un-American." Government, the media, and schools were purged of "subversives." Fear of that label led many prominent African Americans to distance themselves from left-wingers. The Federal Bureau of Investigation under J. Edgar Hoover (no supporter of civil rights) devoted considerable resources to investigating possible links between civil rights organizers, such as Martin Luther King, Jr., and persons the Bureau regarded as disloyal. At the same time the FBI refused aid to civil rights activists who were subjected to unlawful threats and violence. Instead it created a special program called COINTELPRO to undermine organizations promoting civil rights by means ranging from "dirty tricks" to assassinations. Despite these repressive measures, however, domestic pressure built for civil rights.

The discussion so far might have suggested that the Second Reconstruction stemmed primarily from federal initiatives. That impression would be mistaken. Its foundation was the Civil Rights Movement that emerged into public awareness in the 1950s and 1960s and to which we now turn.

18

THE CIVIL RIGHTS MOVEMENT

It is often suggested that the Civil Rights Movement began, after *Brown v. Board of Education* was decided, with the Montgomery, Alabama, bus boycott of 1955–56, during which Martin Luther King, Jr., emerged as a dignified and charismatic leader. That view ignores the many campaigns for civil rights that developed along with America's color line, some of which we noted in earlier chapters. Here we shall recall several civil rights campaigns, beginning with one that led to the Supreme Court's decision in *Brown*.

The Moton High School Boycott

The underfunded and overcrowded Moton High School which served black students in Prince Edward County, Virginia, had grossly inadequate facilities that were markedly inferior to the county's Farmville High School for white students. In the fall of 1950 sixteen-year-old Barbara Johns began assembling a group of her fellow Moton students, who then carefully planned a student strike to protest the Jim Crow disparities. When the strike was called in the spring, it was supported overwhelmingly by Moton's students. Moton's principal, the school superintendent, and leaders of the local NAACP tried to persuade the students to end the strike. After all, Jim Crow practice put seriously at risk anyone challenging that system, which in this case would predictably extend to the students' parents. But the students were determined to continue and they won over their parents as well as the NAACP. They continued the strike for the remainder of the school year and, with NAACP and parental support, they initiated a suit for school desegregation: *Davis v. County School Board of Prince Edward County* became one of the five cases that were consolidated and decided together as *Brown v. Board of Education*.

The 1951 Moton strike foreshadowed subsequent developments in the Civil Rights Movement, which included many actions by high school and college students. It is easy to see why students might play a significant role. Adults were more likely to be responsible for the daily care and support of others and were less free to take action that might lead to their jailing, firing, or worse. History tells us, of course, that many adults were also involved in civil rights campaigns.

The Montgomery Bus Boycott

The best known civil rights action following the *Brown* decision began on Thursday, December 1, 1955, in Montgomery, Alabama, when Rosa Parks was arrested for refusing to comply with a bus driver's order to give up the seat she lawfully occupied on a segregated bus so that a late-arriving white passenger could sit separately from black passengers.

Ms. Parks's peaceful defiance was no doubt related to the widely publicized *Brown* decision, but it was probably influenced more directly by other events. Parks was an active member of the NAACP's local chapter and was aware of unsuccessful attempts to negotiate reforms of Montgomery's Jim Crow bus system that sought to end practices that were not required by Jim Crow laws, such as gross discourtesy to black passengers by white bus drivers, infrequent stops in black neighborhoods (which provided the vast majority of the city's bus riders), and the absence of black drivers. Parks also knew of deliberations about prior contemplated challenges to that system.

Four days before her own civil disobedience, Ms. Parks attended a mass meeting about three unpunished murders of African Americans that had recently occurred in the neighboring state of Mississippi. The first, in May 1955, was the assassination of George Lee, a fearless voting rights activist who refused to bend under pressure. The second, in mid-August 1955, was the killing of Lamar Smith, also a voting rights activist, who was shot at close range on the busy public lawn in front of a county courthouse. Witnesses to neither murder were available – not even witnesses of the second, public killing – and no one was charged in either case.

Later that same month a young black teenager named Emmett Till was lynched in rural Mississippi. Visiting from Chicago, and either unfamiliar with Jim Crow mores or unappreciative of the possible penalties for violations of them, Till is reported to have spoken briefly to or to have whistled at a white woman. A few days later he was taken from his great-uncle's cabin by the woman's husband and another relative to be brutally beaten, mutilated, and murdered.

After Till's body was discovered, the culprits were identified without difficulty and, seemingly for appearance's sake, were charged and put on trial. Widespread news of the crime led many reporters and a black congressman from Till's home state of Michigan to observe the trial. Despite clear evidence of their guilt, the killers were quickly acquitted. Till's mother had his body returned to Chicago for an open-casket funeral so that others would see his terrible condition (how brutally he was murdered), photos of which were widely circulated.

Rosa Parks's refusal to move further back in the segregated Montgomery bus had not been planned in advance, but her quietly defiant action occurred against the background just described. On the Sunday following her arrest, an overflow meeting of Montgomery's black citizens unanimously agreed to hold a one-day bus boycott in protest. That night, Jo Ann Robinson of the Women's Political Council ran off thousands of leaflets announcing the boycott and had them distributed by the next morning.

As a result, very few African Americans rode the Montgomery buses that Monday – or on any other day for more than a year, as that evening the community decided to continue the boycott indefinitely. Maintaining the action took a high degree of organization as well as much daily sacrifice. It ended only when the city received and complied with the Supreme Court's order to desegregate the buses, under *Browder v. Gayle* (1956).

The Montgomery bus boycott received a great deal of attention, perhaps because of its timing, the character of its principal figures (especially Ms. Parks and Dr. King), the determination of a large, unified black community, and a recognition by many persons of its potential importance. King understood that dismantling Jim Crow would take a number of mass efforts like the Montgomery campaign and that the success of one such action would make others easier to organize. Supporters of the color line saw any such encroachment as a threat to Jim Crow as a whole.

The Supreme Court's *Brown* decision against public school segregation had suggested that the Court was prepared to rule more broadly against Jim Crow, as indeed it did in the Montgomery bus case. Defenders of the system were alarmed. "White Citizens Councils" were organized throughout the South for the express purpose of exerting economic pressure against those who supported *Brown* and sought its extension. More than a hundred members of Congress signed the "Southern Manifesto" endorsing "massive resistance" to "forced integration by any lawful means." The Klan was revived, which made it clear (if anyone needed such clarification) that resistance to civil rights reform would not be limited to lawful or nonviolent measures.

It could not have been surprising to black Southerners that defenses of Jim Crow would include lethal violence. Violence had been one of the principal responses by white supremacists to Reconstruction efforts after the Civil War, it had helped to reestablish racial subjugation after the abolition of slavery, and it was needed to maintain Jim Crow. Violent enforcement of the system was accepted and employed by respectable Southern citizens and by state and local officials and was tolerated by the federal government. Police rarely interfered with unlawful violence against civil rights activists, they routinely arrested peaceful, nonviolent demonstrators, and they often participated in the unlawful violence themselves, sometimes with lethal effect.

Shortly after the Montgomery campaign began, King's house was bombed. When the city's bus system was finally desegregated, his home was bombed again. A year later bombs destroyed the home and the church of King's close associate Ralph Abernathy, as well as two other black churches and the home of another black minister.

King and others worked hard to discourage violent responses by African Americans to the bombings and other violence against civil rights activists. It is easy to understand why, aside from moral objections to violent means. As African Americans were outnumbered and outgunned, King believed that responding to violence with violence would be suicidal. Also, as black Southerners would continue to live alongside white Southerners after Jim Crow was dismantled, nonviolence was a way to minimize grounds for long-term resentment.

A judicious use of violence in self-defense is widely regarded as justified, but violent replies to attacks during public civil rights actions were not tolerated by the leadership of most civil rights organizations. Activists participated with the understanding that they were risking not just their freedom but their lives when they sought to secure rights that they were supposedly guaranteed by law. In the next chapter, we will note self-defense measures that were taken, despite such reservations.

Lunch Counter Sit-Ins

Stores in Southern cities, including local branches of nationwide chains such as Woolworth's, observed Jim Crow practices that were not required by Jim Crow laws, such as limiting black workers to menial jobs and serving only white customers at their lunch counters. Sit-in campaigns that were initiated and conducted mainly by local college students began to challenge those practices.

On February 1, 1960 Joseph McNeil, Franklin McCain, Ezell Blair, Jr., and David Richmond, freshmen at North Carolina Agricultural and Technical State University, asked for service at the lunch counter in Greensboro's Woolworth store. They were refused, but they stayed at the counter until the store closed. They returned the next day, along with other students, reporters, and a TV cinematographer. Increasing numbers of students came to sit-in at the lunch counter for the same purpose each successive day. Sit-ins spread to Greensboro's Kress store and to stores in other North Carolina cities as well as other Southern states.

Those sitting-in at lunch counters were heckled, subjected to abuse, sometimes attacked violently, sometimes arrested for trespass, but in almost all cases they managed to maintain nonviolent discipline. Boycotts of the unresponsive stores were organized, affecting sales so much that within months the stores desegregated their lunch counters.

These were not the first lunch counter sit-ins aimed at desegregating public facilities. During the summer of 1958 sit-ins had successfully desegregated stores in Wichita, Kansas, and Oklahoma City. In the same year, students from several colleges in Nashville, Tennessee, attended workshops on nonviolent means of challenging segregation. The following year, local civil rights leaders asked Nashville department store owners to desegregate their lunch counters, with no success. That fall the students tried out brief sit-ins at local stores, with predictable responses. When word came in February of the Greensboro sit-ins, the Nashville students decided to proceed with their own. From the start hundreds participated, in several stores. When police were not present, white hecklers turned violent, after which scores of students who participated in the sit-ins were arrested. The home of the lawyer who headed the team that represented the Nashville students was bombed.

Nashville's black religious leaders supported the students' actions and initiated a boycott of stores in the city that maintained Jim Crow practices. The boycott persuaded the stores to test the desegregation of lunch counters, which proceeded without incident. The boycott was ended and Nashville lunch counters were desegregated peacefully. Desegregation of other public facilities in Nashville did not occur, however, until it was mandated by the Civil Rights Act of 1964. The student leaders of the Nashville actions included John Lewis and Diane Nash, who soon joined and helped lead other civil rights actions, such as the 1961 Freedom Rides.

One of the most important organizers of the period was Ella Baker, who in 1960 was director of the Southern Christian Leadership Conference SCLC, which had been organized by Reverend King after the Montgomery bus boycott. Recognizing the significance of the student-run sit-in campaigns, Ms. Baker organized a conference of student activists for April of that year. The Student Nonviolent Coordinating Committee was then born. SNCC became the organizing center for the most difficult and dangerous actions in the Deep South, including the continuation of the Freedom Rides and the voter registration campaign in Mississippi.

Freedom Rides

The Supreme Court's 1946 decision in *Morgan v. Virginia* outlawed racial segregation on interstate buses. Compliance with that decision was tested by an inter-racial group from the Congress of Racial Equality in the 1947 "Journey of Reconciliation." Although they limited their journey to the Upper South, they were nevertheless arrested and imprisoned. No federal agency or official intervened on their behalf.

In 1955 the Interstate Commerce Commission ruled in the *Sarah Keys* case against racial segregation in bus travel between states, and in 1960 the Supreme Court ruled in *Boynton v. Virginia* against racial segregation in bus terminals, but the ICC made no effort to enforce those decisions. The Freedom Rides of 1961 challenged their violation in the Deep South.

The Freedom Riders came from CORE and SNCC. One group traveled by Greyhound, another by Trailways. Black and white participants sat together, other black members of the group sat in the front of the bus, and other white members sat in the back. In traveling south, they were met with arrests and severe beatings that were organized or facilitated by local police. One of the buses was firebombed in Mississippi. Images of the burning bus and of badly beaten participants were sent around the world. (President Kennedy's reaction was to call the Freedom Riders unpatriotic for embarrassing America.)

As a result of the nearly fatal incidents, the first set of Freedom Rides was cut short. Determined not to let violent segregationists nullify reform rulings by the Supreme Court, Diane Nash immediately organized new Freedom Rides from Nashville to Birmingham, where the Riders were arrested and jailed. When they resumed the Rides, they faced similar treatment. Nevertheless, scores of Freedom Rides took place throughout that summer and fall. Hundreds of black and white individuals participated, and all were arrested. In September of 1961, under belated pressure from the Kennedy administration, the ICC finally issued desegregation orders which went into effect that November. People of color would no longer be subjected to humiliating and degrading interstate travel facilities. Federal action was necessary, but there was no prospect of it until the Freedom Rides were conducted by CORE and SNCC.

Birmingham

Birmingham was known as the most segregated city in America, and its principal method of enforcement earned it the nickname "Bombingham." The Birmingham campaign of 1962–63 was designed to desegregate the city's main public facilities, including its privately owned downtown department stores. Early in the campaign a boycott led a number of the stores to promise desegregation, but threats from Eugene "Bull" Connor, Birmingham's Commissioner of Public Safety, caused them to renege on the agreement. The campaign then resumed, with boycotts of downtown stores, marches to the voting registrar, sit-ins at libraries and lunch counters, and "kneel-ins" at churches.

In 1963 King came to Birmingham at the invitation of Fred Shuttlesworth, head of the local affiliate of the Southern Christian Leadership Conference. King and others marched despite an injunction that Connor had secured from a local judge. Scores of marchers were arrested and King was kept isolated in the Birmingham jail from which he issued his famous "Letter from Birmingham City Jail," explaining the issues and defending the campaign.

Organizers who were not in jail, including Dorothy Cotton and James Bevel, then initiated a "Children's Crusade," involving black high school students (and even some in elementary school). The youngsters took nonviolence workshops and then hundreds of them, in disciplined groups of fifty, marched peacefully, two abreast, from the Sixteenth Street Baptist Church towards City Hall, until they were stopped, arrested, and taken to jail, which they soon filled. Connor tried to stop the second day's flow of young marchers by ordering firemen to direct high pressure streams of water at them, while police dogs attacked marchers and black bystanders. With Connor's brutal tactics in full view, support for the campaign within the black community increased immediately. Nor was the effect merely local: televised images of the assaults on children were transmitted around the world (to the consternation of President Kennedy).

The Children's Crusade lasted five days and achieved its objective of forcing influential members of the city's white community to negotiate. Despite resistance from local politicians, a desegregation agreement was eventually reached. Federal troops were called in to replace aggressive state police, and desegregation was initiated. Kennedy went on television to call for new civil rights legislation, which eventually became the Civil Rights Act of 1964, enacted, after Kennedy's assassination in Texas, under his successor, Lyndon Johnson.

During the campaign, bombs destroyed Fred Shuttlesworth's home and church; the home of Martin Luther King's brother, A.D. King; the Gaston Motel, where King had stayed; and the home of an NAACP attorney. Shortly after Birmingham's schools were desegregated in fall 1964, a bomb exploded in the Sixteenth Street Baptist Church, killing four young black girls – Addie Mae Collins, Denise McNair, Carole Robertson, and Cynthia Wesley.

That unconscionable act followed another – the assassination of Medgar Evers, head of the Mississippi NAACP, who had been busy developing a desegregation campaign in the state capital of Jackson. Evers's life had been constantly under threat. As he returned home one evening, he was gunned down in the driveway of his house.

Later that summer, the March on Washington for Jobs and Freedom brought a quarter of a million people of all colors to the nation's capital. It was there that King gave his famous "I Have a Dream" speech. The support for civil rights represented by the march may have helped promote passage of the following year's Civil Rights Act. But its surface unity obscured its exclusion of speeches by women who were leaders of the movement as well as statements critical of the Kennedy administration's weak support for civil rights.

Freedom Summer

In 1962 President Kennedy and his brother Robert, the Attorney General, persuaded several foundations to fund a Voter Education Project, which the Kennedys thought would generate less unfavorable publicity for the United States than direct action campaigns like the 1961 Freedom Rides. As voter registration was a central aim of civil rights organizations, four national groups agreed to collaborate in the project, concentrating on Mississippi. CORE would do field work in one of the state's congressional districts, SNCC would be responsible for the other four districts, the SCLC would run a citizenship school program, and the NAACP would provide legal support. A new Council of Federated Organizations (COFO) would coordinate their activities, with Robert Parris (Bob) Moses as Project Director.

For civil rights, Mississippi was Birmingham writ large. Less than 1% of the state's eligible African Americans were registered to vote.

Even before the Voter Education Project was begun, in 1961 Bob Moses had moved from New York to McComb, Mississippi, to begin SNCC's voter registration project there. Moses was committed to the development of broad black participation and respect for local black leadership. Like other SNCC field workers, he depended on the black communities in which he worked for support such as housing. SNCC organizers moved frequently, for the sake of their hosts, because the homes and churches that extended hospitality to civil rights workers were subject to firebombing.

The voting rights campaigners were greeted with beatings, arrests, and murder. The first victim of this campaign was Herbert Lee. He had worked with Bob Moses and was killed in 1961. Louis Allen, who had witnessed Lee's killing, was murdered in 1964.

Allard Lowenstein, a white supporter of the voting rights campaign, had suggested to Moses the idea of bringing white college students to work on voter registration in Mississippi, and Moses thought the publicity that would be generated by such a project would help. After a trial run of that arrangement in 1963, Freedom Summer was initiated for 1964. More than a thousand volunteers were recruited, mostly white college students from Northern campuses, to join with thousands of African Americans from Mississippi. The volunteers were screened to ensure that they were prepared to work under local black leaders.

An orientation session was held at an Ohio college campus in June 1964. While it was proceeding, COFO reported that three field workers had failed to report in as they regularly did. James Earl Chaney, Andrew Goodman, and Michael Schwerner had gone to inspect the ruins of a black church that had been burned down after being opened to civil rights activities. At the orientation Moses informed those present of the fears for the three who were missing. None of the volunteers decided to withdraw.

The FBI refused to do anything about the missing men until they were ordered by the Attorney General to do so. For several weeks a search was conducted. The searchers discovered bodies of several other African Americans, at least three of whom could be identified as civil rights activists. With the aid of informants, the three missing voting rights workers' bodies were found buried in an earthen dam, and the circumstances were also revealed. The three had been arrested, released, and turned over to Klansmen who killed the two white men and beat Chaney brutally before killing him.

The news shocked the nation. Goodman's and Schwerner's families noted pointedly how the public expressed outrage at the killing of two white men while murders of black civil rights workers had no comparable effect. Mississippi did not prosecute the accused, but they were later charged and convicted of federal crimes under an 1870 statute. The Civil Rights Act of 1964 finally got through the US

Senate, despite a lengthy Southern filibuster, and was signed into law by President Johnson in early July.

Freedom Summer proceeded with programs that supplemented voter registration efforts. Dozens of voluntary Freedom Schools were conducted in churches, community centers, and private homes. Thousands attended, most but not all of grade school age. The curriculum centered on English and mathematics but also included subjects like black history and civil rights.

Still, few African Americans were allowed to register as voters. As the state's Democratic Party continued to exclude African Americans, another Freedom Summer project was initiated to provide an inclusive alternative. The creation was called the Mississippi Freedom Democratic Party, which was run according to Democratic Party rules without racial exclusions. In due course, the MFDP elected delegates to the national Democratic Party convention that was scheduled for August, where it would challenge the credentials of the Jim Crow state delegation.

At the convention, MFDP delegates made a persuasive case before the Credentials Committee – an especially powerful case, when the Committee was addressed by Fannie Lou Hamer, a former sharecropper who had been driven from her home and severely beaten because of her voting rights work. The proceedings were televised, and President Johnson, who still hoped for some support from Southern Democrats, intervened to prevent the unseating of the all-white Mississippi delegation and preempted TV coverage of the Credentials Committee proceedings with a hastily arranged presidential address. The MFDP was offered two seats without votes, and turned them down. Most of the Jim Crow delegation from Mississippi walked out anyway, but the MFDP was not permitted to replace them.

This experience, added to the bias pointed out by Goodman's and Schwerner's families, intensified frustration and bitterness, especially among black activists – reactions that would be reinforced the following year in Selma, Alabama.

The Selma Campaign

In the late 1950s African Americans in Selma had organized the Dallas County Voters League to promote the registration of black men and women, where fewer than 1% of the eligible black voters were registered. Facing intense resistance, they made little progress. SNCC field workers who joined them in 1963 were subjected to beatings and arrests. When a judge issued an injunction against any meeting of three or more persons to discuss civil rights, the DCVL asked for additional help from King. In late 1964 the SCLC sent several organizers, including Diane Nash and James Bevel.

The following March state troopers attacked a voting rights march to nearby Marion and killed a young black participant, Jimmie Lee Jackson. As a way of focusing anger constructively, it was decided to conduct a march from Selma to

Montgomery, the state capital, where a protest rally would be held. The plan was condemned by Governor Wallace who ordered that it be prevented.

On March 7 several hundred peaceful marchers leaving Selma were attacked by state troopers, some on horseback, with clubs and tear gas. They knocked down many marchers and caused serious injuries. The ghastly scene, which was televised to a shocked international audience, has since been known as "Bloody Sunday."

King sent out a call for others to join a new march on March 9, and hundreds came from across the country. But a federal judge ordered a delay. On the day of the march King turned around the marchers shortly after the march had begun – to much consternation, as King had not discussed that plan with many of the co-organizers. Those who had traveled far to join the march were asked to stay for a third attempt.

That evening three clergy who had answered King's call were attacked on a Selma street. The Reverend James Reeb from Boston died from his wounds two days later. Once again, there was a shocked reaction whereas little notice had been taken of Jimmie Lee Jackson's murder, which had been the occasion for the march. Reeb was white, Jackson was black. The color line continued to regulate white America's compassion.

On March 15 President Johnson gave a televised speech to a joint session of Congress in which he proposed the Voting Rights Act, which Congress enacted and he signed into law later that summer.

Meanwhile the federal judge sanctioned a third march and lifted his earlier restraining order. The march began on March 16, and at its termination on the 25th twenty-five thousand gathered for a rally in Montgomery.

That evening Viola Liuzzo of Detroit was killed by Klan gunfire while ferrying marchers between the two cities. The FBI then spread false rumors about her, so less distress was registered over her murder.

Murders of civil rights activists continued throughout the period. For example: Jonathan Daniels, a seminary student from Boston, was arrested, released, and shot in Hayneville, Alabama, on August 20, 1965. Student Samuel Younge, Jr., was shot in Tuskegee, Alabama, on January 3, 1966. The home of Vernon Dahmer of Hattiesburg, Mississippi, was firebombed on January 10, 1966, and he later died of his injuries. Clarence Triggs of Bogalusa, Louisiana, was shot on July 30, 1966. Wharlest Jackson of Natchez, Mississippi, died on February 27, 1967, from a bomb that had been planted in his car. Samuel Hammond, Jr., Delano Middleton, and Henry Smith were shot and killed by police during a demonstration at the South Carolina State College campus in Orangeburg on February 8, 1968. On April 4, 1968 Martin Luther King, Jr., was shot and killed in Memphis, Tennessee, where he was supporting a strike of black sanitation workers. Along with King and those who are listed above, one hundred and seven others who were sacrificed to the color line between 1954 and 1968 are named at the civil rights memorial that was established two decades later in Montgomery, Alabama.

19

BLACK SEPARATISM, ARMED SELF-DEFENSE, AND URBAN DISORDERS

The picture provided so far of African America following World War II has omitted some major figures, such as Malcolm X, some important organizations, such as the Black Panthers, some issues that divided the Civil Rights Movement, such as "Black Power," and any acknowledgment of urban disorders (events that some refer to as "riots" and others refer to as "uprisings" or "rebellions"). This chapter fills some of the gaps in the previous narrative.

While Malcolm Little was in prison for crimes against property, he joined the Nation of Islam, an exclusively black religious group, and became Malcolm X. Upon his parole in 1952, Malcolm X became active in the NOI and was soon its most effective organizer and most articulate public figure. Within the black community Malcolm X's critique of American society was regarded as most accurately depicting the color line along with the white community's pretensions and hypocrisy.

Malcolm X demonstrated his leadership in 1957 as head of the Nation's Harlem Temple Number 7. After members of the Temple had been beaten and arrested by New York City policemen, Malcolm X sought to see them. When the police denied that those who had been arrested were being held at the police station, Malcolm X rapidly mobilized several hundred (ultimately several thousand) "Black Muslims" who assembled silently outside the station. The police were persuaded, and Malcolm X's request was granted.

Although it was a peaceful, nonviolent action, it was also coercive – as could be said of many nonviolent "direct" political actions, such as boycotts and sit-ins. Nonviolent political actions are often coercive. Reform movements could not advance without employing such pressure, which King called "creative tension."

For most of his public career, Malcolm X rejected equality and integration. Why would one wish to associate with the "white devils" who had proved brutal, oppressive, exploitative, and genocidal?

In the last year of his life, however, after leaving the Nation of Islam and receiving respectful treatment by Muslims of all colors during his pilgrimage to Mecca, Malcolm X endorsed racial equality and, most significantly, offered his support to King. That promising new stage of his political career was cut short by his assassination on February 1, 1965. Malcolm X was mourned by many respected black figures from James Baldwin to Martin Luther King, Jr.

One thing that distinguished Malcolm X from King and other civil rights leaders was his advocacy of securing human rights for African Americans "by any means necessary." He rejected an absolute commitment to nonviolence and criticized civil rights leaders for passively accepting violent responses to their political actions. Self-defense, he insisted, is as principled as it is necessary.

Others agreed. Despite public controversy surrounding the idea, armed self-defense became an important component of the Civil Rights Movement.

In Monroe, North Carolina, the Ku Klux Klan openly used guns to resist the desegregation of public facilities and intimidate the black community. The local police declined even to take notice of Klan actions. In the mid-1950s, Robert F. Williams, a black veteran of the US Marines and head of the local NAACP, organized, effectively employed, and articulately defended armed self-defense. Williams did not initiate violence, but armed self-defense by African Americans was too much for the white establishment to accept. In 1961 Williams and his wife were falsely charged with kidnapping a white couple who they had protected from a mob, and as a result they fled abroad. (After they returned in 1969, North Carolina dropped all charges against them.) At Williams's funeral in 1996, Rosa Parks, speaking, as she said, on behalf of those who had struggled for civil rights in Montgomery, Alabama, praised Williams's work in Monroe.

Williams was not alone. In 1964 an armed self-defense group, the Deacons for Defense and Justice, was organized in Jonesboro, Louisiana, to protect civil rights activists and their communities against Klan violence. The Deacons developed twenty-one chapters in Alabama, Louisiana, and Mississippi. For good reason.

To see the Deacons in their proper context it will be helpful to step back in time once again. During the 1960s, despite official resistance and violent rioting by defenders of the color line, desegregation was begun at universities in the Deep South. The career of one trailblazer, James Meredith, is especially relevant here. In 1962 the University of Mississippi found itself legally obliged to accept Meredith as its first African American student. Mississippi's legislature and its governor Ross Barnett then threw up what official roadblocks they could to Meredith's studying at "Ole Miss." These were soon legally dismantled, but the official resistance to Meredith's attendance encouraged violent mobs of white supremacists to assemble on the campus. Federal troops were called in to end their rioting, during which much property was destroyed and two persons were killed.

Despite considerable harassment, Meredith studied that year at the University of Mississippi, completed his degree, and then undertook postgraduate studies abroad. After returning to the US, Meredith embarked in 1966 on a solo "March

Against Fear" to Jackson, Mississippi, from Memphis, Tennessee, in order to support voter registration and draw attention to the slow pace of civil rights progress. Although Meredith had been assured of state police protection, he was shot on the second day of his march. Civil rights organizations decided at once to continue the march on his behalf. Thousands participated and Meredith, who had been hospitalized, was able to rejoin the march before it reached Jackson.

During the march, at the urging of Stokely Carmichael, then chairman of SNCC, leaders of the represented civil rights organizations agreed to have the Deacons provide armed defense. The Deacons' quiet presence may well have prevented the need for their active service. As Malcolm X had insisted, nonviolence does not exclude self-defense.

The 1966 march was noteworthy for another reason. Nonviolent campaigns for civil rights had cost many their lives, but their sacrifices had not much changed the conditions of black life in America, while violent resisters continued to act with impunity. Frustration was increasingly expressed. One evening, in a speech at an encampment along the route to Jackson, Carmichael – a veteran civil rights campaigner who had experienced more than his share of arrests, beatings, and jailings – called emphatically for "Black Power." This was not the first time that expression had been used, but it became the best known. It is of interest here not so much for what Carmichael personally meant as for what it variously came to mean inside and outside the Movement – which included black pride, black self-defense, and black separatism. For SNCC it came to mean the exclusion of whites, expressing less a distrust of SNCC's own white activists than an insistence on black organizational independence and a widely shared frustration with the slow, if not stalled, character of civil rights reform.

That brings us to some of the more controversial aspects of the 1960s. One of the twentieth century's outstanding athletes, Cassius Clay, won a gold medal for boxing at the 1960 Olympics. After the Olympics, Clay converted to Islam. In 1964 Clay became heavyweight boxing champion, changed his name to Muhammad Ali, and joined the Nation of Islam. Two years later Ali refused induction into the US military on religious grounds as well as opposition to the American war in Vietnam. He said, in effect, that he had no argument with the Vietnamese but with the color line in America. After Ali's application for conscientious objector status was denied, he was charged, tried, and convicted of violating the Selective Service law. Ali was stripped of his boxing titles and barred from competition until his conviction was overturned by the US Supreme Court in 1967.

Ali's anti-war position may well have influenced growing opposition to American military intervention in Southeast Asia, an opposition that King himself openly expressed in 1967, to the great discomfort of more moderate, or more intimidated, civil rights leaders. Although Ali was known for deliberately provocative public pronouncements, he was also widely respected for his principled position on the war.

It is interesting to compare Ali's public persona with that of Jackie Robinson two decades earlier. At great personal cost, Robinson had been obliged to tolerate vicious verbal abuse when he challenged major league baseball's color line. By contrast, Ali was an outspoken champion of black pride and independence.

But how much had conditions changed for the black community? As the President's Committee on Civil Rights reported in the 1940s, housing, education, jobs, the legal system, and public policy were regulated by the color line. By the 1960s not much had changed.

Discriminatory police conduct, including lethal brutality against African Americans, was an especially visible component of the color line. (At the time of writing, in 2019, that has not changed.) It sometimes precipitated expressions of black frustration that shocked the white community. Beginning in 1964, urban disorders, mainly sparked by police misconduct, broke out in a number of Northern black ghettos. Some lasted for days. All told, they resulted in sixty thousand arrests, ten thousand serious injuries, and two hundred and fifty deaths.

A National Advisory Commission on Civil Disorders, chaired by Illinois governor Otto Kerner, was appointed by President Johnson in 1967. In its 1968 report, the Kerner Commission stressed the responsibility of "white society" for the creation and maintenance of the black urban ghetto. The Commission observed that "Our nation is moving toward two societies, one black, one white – separate and unequal" – which seemed to understate the conditions that were described by the Commission. Its report called for "the realization of common opportunities for all" through a set of programs that required "unprecedented levels of funding and performance." Its recommendations regarding jobs, schools, housing, and income support did not differ much from those that had earlier been advanced by the Black Panthers (see below) and are not yet outdated. Such positive recommendations would soon be displaced by a federal focus on "crime control" and a "War on Drugs."

The Black Panther Party for Self-Defense had been founded in 1966, primarily to monitor police activities, for which it deployed openly armed patrols. Although the Panthers are understood to have embraced a radical perspective, their "Ten Point Program" called basically for political and economic reforms that would be substantial enough to extinguish the color line and create equal opportunity, so that the life prospects of black and white children would be substantially the same. From Oakland, California, the Panthers expanded to scores of Northern cities where they developed "survival programs," such as free breakfasts for children, free medical clinics, and clothing distribution. The Panthers' early positions and activities attracted considerable support in the white as well as black communities.

The Panthers' complex history, which remains controversial, cannot be reviewed fully here. It is well established, however, that the Panthers were greatly affected by an intensive FBI (COINTELPRO) campaign aimed at destroying the organization by any means necessary, which ranged from dirty tricks to assassinations of Panther organizers, such as Fred Hampton, who was killed, along with fellow Panther Mark Clark, by Chicago police in an operation initiated by the FBI in 1969.

20

THE WIDER CIVIL RIGHTS MOVEMENT

As America's color line includes more hues than black and white, so did the Civil Rights Movement that emerged after World War II. Its segments differed in their histories, their most pressing issues, and their actions.

Consider for a moment the matter of US citizenship. Despite the birthright citizenship clause of the Fourteenth Amendment, until the Indian Citizenship Act of 1924 the federal government did not officially regard Native Americans as US citizens, presumably on the ground that they were not "subject to the jurisdiction of" the United States – a notion that clashed with increasing federal intervention in tribal affairs. Unsurprisingly, the conferral of citizenship did not engender respect by the federal government for treaty-based rights of many indigenous communities (e.g., to territory and annuities), which were often violated and sometimes nullified by legislative or administrative action.

Most Mexican Americans were US citizens, but one would not have inferred that from government policies. The same 1848 treaty that conferred American citizenship on residents of the Mexican Cession supposedly guaranteed their land rights, for example, but most such rights were soon lost. One promising post-World War II development was the successful challenge of school segregation by Mexican Americans in *Mendez v. Westminister* (1947), several years before the Supreme Court outlawed school segregation more generally in *Brown v. Board of Education*.

Because the US and China had become war-time allies, in 1943 the US reversed course and allowed Chinese Americans to become citizens. But it did not do the same for all other residents of color, and federal courts still upheld state laws that denied "aliens" who were "ineligible for US citizenship" the right to own land.

War-time propaganda had emphasized an American commitment to democracy and racial equity. Those ideas, plus military service by many Americans of color (including some Japanese Americans who had been interned), led to increasing militancy against discrimination within communities of color.

And the black Civil Rights Movement clearly influenced other American communities. The lunch counter sit-ins in the South were soon followed, for example, by "fish-ins" in the Northwest to assert Indian treaty rights; Stokely Carmichael's demand for Black Power was echoed in a call for "Red Power" by the Native American scholar-activist Vine Deloria; and the Black Panthers' street patrols to monitor police activities in Oakland inspired patrols in Minneapolis by the American Indian Movement.

Let's now look more closely at civil rights activities by the several communities of color and their background.

Native America

By the beginning of the twentieth century, most Indian land had been expropriated, Indian nations had been consigned to reservations, the government's allotment program had reduced Indian landholdings even further, and the termination program was ending federal recognition of Indian nations along with treaty obligations to them. Warfare, dislocation, economic privation, and disease had reduced the indigenous population of North America from more than ten million to a quarter of a million. Boarding schools were imposing European ways upon those Native American children who had managed to survive, as the framers of federal Indian policy continued to assume that Native Americans needed cultural whitening, if they were to be saved – should that even be possible.

The Native American children in a given boarding school might be sent or taken from several different Indian communities. As a result, friendships that formed among inmates of the schools led later to inter-tribal cooperation. In 1911 alumni from the schools – Native American professionals who had been educated in white institutions – founded the Society of American Indians – the first national organization not only *for* Indians but *of* them. The Society sought US citizenship for Native Americans and a legal process for hearing claims against the federal government.

The Society's central aims were achieved, but not until after it had ceased to function. Congress enacted the Indian Citizenship Act in 1924, and the Indian Claims Commission was established in 1946, partly through the efforts of the National Congress of American Indians. Founded in 1944, the NCAI engaged in lobbying and litigation on issues ranging from the enforcement of Indian rights to jobs, education, and health care.

Dissatisfied with the NCAI's limited modes of action, Indian college students and recent graduates founded the National Indian Youth Council in 1961. The Council focused first on tribal fishing rights that were being denied by the states in violation of federal treaties. It joined a campaign that was begun in 1954 when an Indian fisherman was arrested for failing to comply with state regulations that ignored Indian fishing rights. The Council's assistance led to a 1964 "fish-in" attended by thousands from dozens of Indian communities along with prominent white supporters. Many participants were arrested. The fishing rights campaign continued until the US Supreme Court in 1974 confirmed the Indians' treaty-based entitlements.

Founded in 1968, the American Indian Movement was committed to addressing a range of Native American issues. Working first with urban Indians, AIM established police-monitoring patrols in Minneapolis. Before we recount more of AIM's history, however, we must take note of the single most galvanizing event of the period.

The federal prison on Alcatraz Island in San Francisco Bay had been closed in 1963. A number of Native Americans understood that the Fort Laramie Treaty of 1868 authorized the return to Indians of disused federal property, and that Alcatraz Island qualified. In November 1969 an occupation of the island by "Indians of All Tribes" began with the expressed purpose of establishing a Native American cultural center there. Some participants may have regarded the occupation as a form of street theater aimed at increasing public awareness of issues facing Native Americans. This is suggested by the text of the "Proclamation," which was addressed "To the Great White Father and All His People," claimed the island "by right of discovery," and followed European precedent by offering to purchase it "for twenty-four dollars ($24) in glass beads and red cloth." The Proclamation observed that the island "is more than suitable for an Indian Reservation" as it "resembles most reservations" in being "isolated from modern facilities," lacking industry, with high unemployment and rocky, non-productive soil. Moreover, the "population has always been held as prisoners and kept dependent on others."

The occupation of Alcatraz Island continued for nineteen months. At its peak, participants numbered four hundred, were supported by Americans of various colors, made radio broadcasts, and published a newspaper. In the spring of 1971 the federal government ended the island's telephone service and electrical power supply, and soon after removed the few remaining occupiers. But the Alcatraz occupation appears to have served as an inspiration for potential activists.

Although the American Indian Movement was not much involved in Alcatraz, AIM carried its provocative spirit further. In 1970, for example, it seized the *Mayflower* replica. In 1971 it occupied Mount Rushmore (which resides on Lakota land), the Bureau of Indian Affairs' offices in Washington, DC, and a Wisconsin dam that had flooded Ojibwe territory. In 1972 AIM co-sponsored the Trail of Broken Treaties with the Native American Youth Council and other American Indian organizations, including the Native American Rights Fund (a legal support group, which was founded in 1970). The Trail included a cross-country caravan from the West Coast to Washington, DC. When representatives of the Nixon administration refused to receive the group's Twenty-Point Statement calling for policy reforms, Trail participants occupied the building that housed the Bureau of Indian Affairs, where much damage was done to property and records.

In early 1973 AIM was called to the Oglala Lakota Pine Ridge Reservation in South Dakota by the Oglala Sioux Civil Rights Organization. OSCRO had unsuccessfully sought to impeach the tribal president, whom they accused of corruption and violent abuse of power. Many details of what happened thereafter are controverted, but the following seems clear. OSCRO and AIM (which was already a COINTELPRO target) seized and occupied the town of Wounded Knee on the Pine Ridge Reservation, heavily armed federal forces laid siege to the town, and there was considerable gunfire in both directions, leading to deaths on each side. After seventy-one days, tribal elders decided to end the occupation. The desired reforms were not achieved, the tribal president resumed his position, and violence was intensified on the reservation itself. The following year, the federal prosecution of two AIM leaders on charges relating to the occupation was ended when the court dismissed all charges (after the jury had voted to acquit) because of serious prosecutorial misconduct.

Actions later organized by AIM included the 1978 Longest Walk, from San Francisco to the federal capital, in which many Indian nations were represented, and which thousands joined along the way. The Walk publicized several issues of concern, including proposed legislation that was seen as threatening tribal sovereignty. It would appear to have succeeded, as Congress rejected the proposed abrogation of federal treaties and enacted the American Religious Freedom Restoration Act.

During the post-war period, Native American lobbying and agitation successfully opposed the government's termination policy. Federal recognition was restored for most of the Indian nations that had been terminated, which also restored federal obligations to them. Native American self-determination is once again accepted as a principal feature of federal policy.

Latinos

Mexican Americans have always comprised the majority, by far, of Latinos. They were the original residents of the large territory that was taken from Mexico in 1848, after which Mexicans continued to move back and forth across the newly drawn US–Mexico boundary.

Puerto Ricans have been the second largest Latino community, at least since America's colonization of the island. Shortly after World War II, more than a million Puerto Ricans moved to the mainland, to be followed by many from the Dominican Republic, Cuba, Colombia, El Salvador, Guatemala, and Nicaragua.

The League of United Latin American Citizens, founded in 1929, was for many years the main Latino civil rights organization, centered in the Mexican American communities of the Southwest. LULAC worked for Latino political participation and opposed the poll tax, school segregation, and other forms of discrimination. Its legal work led to important judicial precedents including *Mendez v. Westminster* (previously noted), in which federal courts ruled against the segregation of Mexican American school children.

The League sought the assimilation of Latinos into American society. For LULAC, this meant minimizing if not eliminating cultural differences, by encouraging English usage, for example, and seeking the acceptance of Latinos as white. It also meant stressing the US citizenship of Mexican Americans and opposing Mexican immigration, as the latter encouraged a perception by self-styled white Americans of Latinos as sojourners with little or no stake in American society.

After World War II, many Mexican American military veterans joined LULAC, and in 1948 some founded the American GI Forum. The Forum focused first on veterans' rights, but soon worked for Latinos more generally. Legal initiatives by the Forum and LULAC led to the 1954 case of *Hernandez v. Texas*, in which the Supreme Court held that discrimination against ethnic as well as racial groups violated the equal protection clause.

The idea that Mexican Americans should be considered white was challenged by the Chicano Student Movement of Aztlan, or MEChA, founded in 1969, which held that Latinos are neither black nor white. Expressing pride in a distinctive identity, MEChA embraced "Chicano," which had originally been a term of disparagement.

Many Mexican Americans worked as farm laborers. They lacked union representation, its protections and its benefits. Farm workers' grievances began to be addressed by grassroots organizers in the 1950s, which led to the 1962 formation of the United Farm Workers, centered in California. The UFW organizing campaign faced growers' intransigence and police hostility, but it received wide support during the national grape boycott, begun in 1965, which led to union contracts by 1970.

During this period, other organizations arose in the Mexican American community, including the Young Chicanos for Community Action, who became known as the Brown Berets. The Brown Berets not only sought educational and job opportunities; they also opposed the Vietnam War, supported the UFW, aided Alianza Federal de Mercedes (which sought to recover land taken from Mexicans after 1848), opened health clinics, and joined the short-lived Rainbow Coalition that was organized by the Black Panthers' Fred Hampton and others.

Frustration over school conditions led to the "Chicano Blowouts" of 1968, in which first hundreds then thousands of Latino students in East Los Angeles high schools walked out, protesting educational inequities. The same year saw the founding of the Mexican American Legal Defense and Education Fund. In 1969 a coalition of Mexican American groups formed the National Chicano Moratorium Committee, which organized anti-war protests in a number of cities, from Chicago to the West Coast. Los Angeles police sent tear gas into a peaceful 1971 Moratorium march in East Los Angeles with tens of thousands of participants. Some marchers fought back, property was destroyed, many were injured, many were arrested, and four were killed, including the distinguished journalist Ruben Salazar.

Mexican Americans created a number of other organizations to address discrimination, poverty, and a lack of political representation. For example, the Mexican American Youth Organization, started in 1967, worked effectively on voter registration in South Texas. MAYO and others established the La Raza Unida Party which ran third party candidates in California and Colorado as well as Texas. Several LRUP candidates were elected to local offices. The party evolved into a community organization working for Americans of color more generally in the Southwest.

What Mexican Americans were to the Southwest, Puerto Ricans were to cities in the Northeast and Midwest, though a bit later and on a smaller scale. Puerto Ricans in New York City began to show their political potential with the election of Herman Badillo as Bronx Borough President in 1965.

During the 1960s the Young Lords evolved from a Chicago street gang to an organization centered in New York that worked for civil rights, housing for the poor, and colonial liberation, especially for Puerto Rico. Like the Panthers, they ran a free breakfast program, health centers, day care centers, and classes. They conducted direct action campaigns seeking housing and other services for the poor and endorsed armed self-defense. Such activities made them targets of the COINTELPRO program, with the inevitable consequences.

Asian America

At the start of World War II, Asian Americans derived overwhelmingly from China, Japan, and the Philippines. They could not become citizens unless born in the US, and faced systematic discrimination in all spheres of life. Asian immigration was all but precluded by the Asian Exclusion Act of 1924 and the Tydings McDuffie Act of 1934, the latter ending the free movement of Filipinos to America.

Despite the internment of Japanese Americans from the western states during World War II, the US military recruited Japanese Americans as well as other Asian Americans, but only into narrowly segregated units. As China was a war-time ally, the US ended formal barriers to Chinese immigration and naturalization in 1943 and, in 1946, for Filipinos and South Asians, to whom citizenship was also made available.

Thanks to legal work by the Japanese American Citizens League (founded in 1929), the Supreme Court in 1948 and 1952 nullified state laws that discriminated against aliens ineligible for citizenship. During the Cold War, the Immigration and Naturalization Act of 1965 ended the national origins quotas that had been established earlier in the century – but introduced limits on immigration from other nations of the Americas.

Political agitation within Asian American communities, as in other communities of color, was not led by long-established organizations, such as the Japanese

American Citizens League or the Chinese American Citizens Alliance (begun in 1895), but grew out of student opposition to the American war in Southeast Asia.

Asian American students who participated in anti-war coalitions became dissatisfied with the failure of many white activists to recognize the racist character of the Vietnam War. And, ironically, the failure of white Americans to distinguish among Asians of different ancestries helped lead young Asian Americans to develop an Asian American consciousness and identity. This contributed, in turn, to their promotion of ethnic studies programs and greater representation from communities of color on college faculties and in student bodies.

Those aims were shared with African American, Latino, and Native American students in the San Francisco Bay Area, and led to the Third World Strikes at San Francisco State College (1968–69) and the Berkeley campus of the University of California (1969). These long, complex phenomena (which included much violence, especially by local police) resulted in the creation of a College of Ethnic Studies at San Francisco State and an Ethnic Studies Department at UC Berkeley – academic reforms that would have been long delayed, if not excluded, in the absence of cooperative student activism.

21

LIMITS OF THE SECOND RECONSTRUCTION

As we noted earlier, the First Reconstruction was severely limited in depth and duration. A Radical Republican Congress overrode President Johnson's vetoes of Reconstruction enactments, but it could not overcome the Supreme Court's hostility to egalitarian reform. The same Congress was also unwilling to endorse needed measures such as land reform. By 1877 the Republican Party was prepared to make the political deal that withdrew federal troops from the South, ending major Reconstruction efforts. Significant reforms had been made, especially at the constitutional level, which created an egalitarian potential. But the former slave states were allowed to re-institutionalize black subordination, while the North and West maintained their own stringent versions of Jim Crow.

The Second Reconstruction was likewise limited in depth and duration. Civil rights reforms of the 1960s reflected more of a consensus at the federal level. As America's military opponents during World War II were not only racist but genocidal, American propaganda had promoted wider post-war support for reform. But the new consensus did not result simply from a collective change of heart, and it is doubtful that the greater sensitivity to racism within the white community would alone have resulted in significant reforms. Support for civil rights reflected new political conditions, such as the development of a substantial black vote and the emergence of many new nations of color during the Cold War. In those circumstances, white supremacy was officially condemned and overt discrimination was significantly reduced, while Americans of color achieved much greater access to the ballot box, public office, and jury service, especially in the South.

The limits of white America's commitment to reform were suggested in 1964, however, when a number of Northern states and localities rejected the opportunity to approve fair housing laws. The underlying attitudes were confirmed two years later, when white Northerners expressed great hostility to King, as he sought to extend the desegregation campaign into their communities. Two years further on, the Fair Housing Act of 1968 was an almost empty shell, lacking significant enforcement provisions. When such provisions were added twenty years later, their use was not funded. And after federal courts ruled against racial segregation in public housing projects, federal funding for public housing ceased.

Egalitarian reform was getting too close to home – literally. For many white Americans, it is one thing to allow African Americans equal access to the ballot box and even public accommodations, quite another to accept black families in the neighborhood. As a consequence, residential segregation has hardly been affected by the Second Reconstruction and much the same applies to segregation in the public schools, especially in the North.

These developments coincided with a political realignment at the national level, which exploited opposition to the Second Reconstruction. The 1964 Republican candidate for president, Barry Goldwater, who was openly opposed to civil rights reform, achieved the electoral support of five Southern states that had previously been part of the Democratic Party's perennially reliable "Solid South." Goldwater's campaign initiated the Republican Party's new "Southern Strategy," which sought the support of disaffected whites who favored black subordination. Four years later, the Republican Party reaped the fruits of its new electoral strategy with the election of its presidential candidate, Richard Nixon, who opposed vigorous enforcement of civil rights laws as well as busing of students to schools in order to counteract the effects of residential segregation.

After a disgraced Nixon resigned from office during his second term, following the Watergate scandal, the Democrats briefly retrieved the presidency, but only by nominating Jimmy Carter, a Southerner with no commitment to civil rights. And in 1980 Carter was decisively defeated by the Republican Party candidate, Ronald Reagan, who publicly opposed civil rights legislation, publicly supported "states rights" (which meant massive resistance to desegregation), and pointedly gave a crucial campaign speech near Philadelphia, Mississippi, where the three civil rights workers Chaney, Goodman, and Schwerner had been lynched in 1964.

Just as some Radical Republicans by the mid-1860s had recognized that an effective and lasting Reconstruction required land reform, by the mid-1960s many civil rights activists understood that the color line could not be overcome merely by civil rights reform, but required more radical change – as King argued in his 1967 book *Where Do We Go from Here: Chaos or Community?* But the white America that would not accept residential desegregation could not begin to contemplate the kind of systemic social reconstruction that would end racial stratification. Thus, the reforms of the Second Reconstruction, like the reforms of the First, did not address the deeply entrenched material legacy of the color line (to be sketched below) that flows from both private actions and long-standing public policies. To do so would have required a widespread acknowledgment of wrongdoing, a complete rejection of white supremacy, and substantial restitution.

The importance and persistence of whites' disparaging attitudes towards African Americans are further suggested by public policy developments that outlasted civil rights reforms. These will be discussed in the next chapter, but one example may be mentioned here. In 1996 Congress engaged in what has been termed "welfare reform," which ended federal Aid to Families with Dependent Children. Careful studies have shown that this development reflects a widely shared sentiment among whites that black poverty reflects moral deficiencies of the black community.

Like the First Reconstruction, the Second has had some lasting effects. White supremacy has been officially condemned and *de jure* segregation has ended. Educational and employment opportunities have widened for Americans of color, who now vote and hold public office in unprecedented numbers, throughout the country. Public facilities are generally accessible without color restrictions. Segments of an increasingly diverse American community of color have experienced significant benefits.

But the color line has by no means disappeared.

22

THE PERSISTENCE OF THE COLOR LINE

As we have seen, the Second Reconstruction led to significant progress in the legal recognition and enforcement of civil rights. In Mississippi, for example, the percentage of eligible black voters who were actually registered increased from 6.7% to roughly 60% within five years. That reform is fragile, however, as a number of states are currently taking measures to disfranchise less affluent voters, who are disproportionately people of color, and the Supreme Court has nullified crucial enforcement provisions of the 1965 Voting Rights Act. Furthermore, the reforms have done little to reduce material disadvantages that were imposed upon communities of color in housing, schools, jobs, income, unemployment, medical care, health, life expectancy, family resources, and the like.

Some supporters of civil rights reform may have assumed that the formal acceptance of legal equality would somehow eliminate the legacy of slavery and Jim Crow. But that would have overlooked the entrenchment of material inequities, which civil rights reform never tried to address. It also would have underestimated white America's tacit commitment to the color line. That commitment is most clearly reflected in whites' resistance to residential desegregation and hostility to welfare programs as well as government policies and practices that are superficially "color-blind" but have created massive new racial inequities in law enforcement and are disfranchising citizens of color in ways that are reminiscent of Jim Crow.

Consider the residential segregation of African Americans in the urban North, which is so extreme it is characterized by sociologists as "hyper-segregation." One third of African Americans live in geographically extended urban areas whose residents are almost exclusively black. That degree of segregation and its maintenance over time are unique in American history, something that has not been experienced by any other ethnic or immigrant group.

The persistence of the black urban ghetto appears to result from several factors. One is whites' resistance to desegregated neighborhoods. Realtors continue to exploit that resistance, through "block-busting" and channeling white and black clients into predominantly white and predominantly black communities, respectively; and laws against such practices are not significantly enforced. "Color-blind" zoning restrictions of overwhelmingly white communities, such as minimum lot size and the exclusion of multi-unit housing, effectively excludes less affluent families, which disproportionately affects people of color. Limiting public transportation to such communities reinforces that effect.

The existence of the black urban ghetto affects the quality of everyday life. Although black residential neighborhoods are by no means limited to the poor, poverty and joblessness tend to be concentrated in the ghetto because they are more prevalent among African Americans. The unemployment rate for black workers is double that for white workers, and the black poverty rate is more than double the poverty rate for whites. Under those conditions, schools and public services suffer, and commercial services, such as banks and supermarkets, tend to be absent or inferior. Families look for good schools, but rarely find them in the black urban ghetto. White families have the option of settling elsewhere, in neighborhoods that are effectively closed to African Americans.

The conditions that create and sustain the black urban ghetto contribute to the crucially important wealth gap between black and white families. The median weekly wage of black workers is about two thirds that of white workers, and the median income for black households is about three fifths that of white households. But the life prospects of children depend more on their parents' wealth than on their income. Wealth determines the capacity of one generation to aid the next by promoting economic and social mobility. It can be measured as *net financial assets* (what's owned less what's owed) or alternatively as *available financial resources* (funds available for emergencies as well as for investment in, for example, a business or education; this measure would not include, for example, a car that is owned but that is also essential for transportation, and thus would not normally be converted into cash to pay medical bills). By either measure the median net assets for black families are a small fraction of the median net assets for white families.

Thus, the wealth gap between black families and white families is much greater than the income gap: the net financial assets of the median white family are thirteen times those of the median black family and the difference is even greater for available financial resources (which is needed when, for example, illness or unemployment reduces a family's income). As a result of the wealth gap, there is both more downward mobility and less upward mobility for black children than for white children. And the black–white wealth gap has not been narrowing over the past fifty years.

The family home is the single most important factor contributing to family wealth in America and to the capacity of one generation to pass resources on to the next, improving conditions for the latter. Very few African Americans could acquire assets during slavery, few could acquire assets under Jim Crow, and those who could did so with much more difficulty than did whites with similar incomes and employment. Government policies have promoted home acquisition by whites while inhibiting it for African Americans. The government-approved policy of "red-lining," for example, made mortgage and home improvement loans unavailable in black communities or available only at higher interest rates. Red-lining thus reduced the opportunity for African Americans to acquire, maintain, and improve homes. African Americans who could afford the higher interest rates they were charged on housing loans have consequently paid more than whites for homes of similar value, which has reduced their available financial resources for other purposes, such as business ventures or higher education for children. Despite the formal end of practices like red-lining, widespread lending practices continue to make families of color pay more for house purchase and improvement loans than white families of similar financial means. By any measure, black families have accordingly acquired disproportionately less wealth than white families.

In periods of economic hardship, commercial outlets and services withdraw more from poorer communities, buildings fall more frequently into disrepair and are abandoned, and crime increases. These conditions cause housing values to appreciate at a lower rate in black than in white communities, adversely affecting black families' net worth and their ability to borrow in order to invest in educational and business opportunities.

The combined effect of all these factors is profound. Most black children live in households lacking financial assets. Indeed, the vast majority of black children – about four times the proportion of white children – grow up in households that could maintain a subsistence level at the poverty line for only three months if they lost income due to some accident or medical emergency. These disparities have not been decreasing.

We have so far focused on differences between white and black Americans because we have stressed the persistence of hyper-segregation. But systemic disadvantage is not limited to African American communities. Economic conditions for Native Americans are comparable to those for African Americans, including an unemployment rate double that for whites and poverty at about the same rate as for blacks (both varying greatly across the country). Generally speaking, Latinos fare marginally better than African Americans – although considerable differences prevail between, say, Cuban Americans and Dominican Americans, whose respective poverty rates in a recent year were 16.2% and 26.3%. (Because many Cubans emigrated after the 1959 revolution, which the US opposed, Cubans have been uniquely favored among Latinos by official American policies.) A recent study comparing changes in wealth gaps between 2005 (prior to the recent recession) and 2009 found that the median wealth of Hispanic households is only slightly greater than that of black households.

These inequalities are not much affected by the enforcement of anti-discrimination law. Because American history seems to demonstrate that the material inequalities are a legacy of the color line, it is incumbent on American society to address them. But no public policies do so. Instead, current policies exacerbate the inequalities by promoting income and wealth for the most affluent and reducing them for the least advantaged. Effective tax rates tend to be lower for persons in the higher tax brackets, who also fared very well during the recent recession (of 2007–09). Anti-poverty programs that were initiated in the 1960s continue to be cut back, especially during recessions when the needs are greatest.

To put these points in perspective, we might once again consider the life prospects for white and non-white children. The comparison is important because it concerns individuals who could not possibly be considered responsible for such differences. A child of color confronts life prospects that are markedly inferior to those of her white peers. She faces inferior housing, inferior schools, poorer health, fewer job opportunities, greater unemployment, a substantially lower standard of living, less chance of owning a home, less chance of enabling her children to fare better, a shorter life, and, in fact, less chance of surviving infancy. These material differences, combined with the nation's failure to address them, are an affront to the American ideal of equal opportunity.

Let us now turn from the entrenchment of the color line to its current intensi-fication. The same year that Congress enacted the Voting Rights Act, President Johnson announced two "wars" – one on poverty, the other on crime. The War on Poverty involved the expansion of some existing programs, such as Aid to Families with Dependent Children (originally Aid to Dependent Children), and the creation of some new ones, such as Head Start, which helps prepare poor children for school; Section 8 housing vouchers, which cover a portion of rental costs, enabling families to secure affordable housing; and Food Stamps (now the Supplemental Nutrition Assistance Program), which helps families secure subsist-ence levels of nutrition. But the programs were never funded sufficiently to serve all those who qualified for them, many have been scaled back or ended, and none of the programs ever addressed the *causes* of poverty in a wealthy society.

The War on Poverty was displaced by a greatly expanded War on Crime, which evolved under President Reagan into a War on Drugs, which focused on arrests, convictions, and imprisonment. As a result, the number of persons in America who are in prison increased from 1.17 million in 1976 to 5.85 million in 2010. A great deal of the increase results from enforcement and sentencing practices that disproportionately affect African Americans, with further devastating "collateral consequences" for black families and the black community (and with only slightly less disastrous consequences for Latinos).

Here is how this came about. It is well established that drug use occurs at the same frequency within the white and black communities. However, African Americans have been subjected to disproportionately more drug arrests than whites, and prosecutors more frequently offer white defendants than black defendants sig-nificantly reduced plea bargains. Furthermore, the penalty for possession of *one* gram of crack cocaine has, since the 1980s and until recently, been the same as the penalty for *one hundred* grams of powered cocaine, where crack cocaine is more frequently used by African Americans and powdered cocaine is more frequently used by European Americans. (The disparate disadvantage for African Americans was recently reduced from one hundred to one to eighteen to one – still quite substantial, with no good reason for the remaining difference.) These differences have, in turn, greatly contributed to the fact that a much higher proportion of African Americans than European Americans are imprisoned or are under the supervision of the criminal justice system (which includes probation and parole). If current trends continue, one out of every three African American males will be imprisoned in their lifetimes, compared with one out of every six Latinos and one out of every seventeen European Americans.

These unjustifiable differences entail further heavy costs. Persons convicted of felonies (which include most, if not all, of the crimes so far mentioned) are subject to further deprivations mandated by state and federal laws, such as the loss of a professional license (with no connection to the offense), disqualification for educational loans and welfare benefits, and eviction from public housing. Job training and educational opportunities in prison are minimal or non-existent, and employers tend to discriminate against ex-convicts – even against those with only arrest records, no matter if they have been acquitted or the charges were dismissed. The result is that former prisoners have great difficulty securing housing, employment, and the opportunity to become productive members of society.

To these collateral consequences of imprisonment, which are disproportionately visited upon Americans of color, we may add disfranchisement and the resulting disqualification for jury service. Although the federal government has authority to control eligibility to vote in elections for federal offices, state governments regulate voting rights more generally. States have disqualified felons in the past, but these exclusions have been expanded considerably in the past few decades. As a result, today almost 8% of African Americans have been disfranchised by such laws, as opposed to less than 2% of other Americans. While disfranchisement in some states applies only to those in prison, in other states the exclusion is permanent. In the latter states, voting can be restored on an individual basis, but it is very difficult in practice.

We cannot assume that all of these laws and practices were initially intended to disadvantage Americans of color. But they have been subjected to widespread, systematic criticism, which has shown them to have great additional costs and to lack reasonable justifications. The failure to initiate significant reforms encourages the suspicion that their maintenance represents a continued commitment to racial subordination.

This interpretation of current law and social practice is reinforced by the recent addition of voting restrictions in a number of states, such as a requirement that voters show forms of identification that are uncommon for the less affluent, who are disproportionately people of color. (These restrictions affect less affluent whites as well as people of color, but that was also true of poll taxes and other disfranchising devices under Jim Crow.) This interpretation of current law and social practice is reinforced further when the new voting rules are said to prevent voting fraud, which is virtually non-existent in the US, and it seems to be confirmed when some politicians openly embrace the aim of reducing votes for the political party that tends to be favored by Americans of color.

23

WHERE DO WE GO FROM HERE – AND HOW DO WE GET THERE?

To think strategically about how to overcome the color line, we must draw some lessons from America's racial history:

(1) Economic and attitudinal factors together help to explain the color line's creation and persistence. Early on, the most affluent and influential colonists decided that chattel slavery would best serve their economic interests. A highly developed transatlantic slave trade made African slaves available, and this enabled those colonists to reap the economic advantages of slavery, while securing their own political power by giving less affluent whites an interest in maintaining their status above the bottom within a color-coded caste system. Children were socialized to regard people of color as lacking rights, which reinforced any predisposition to regard them as inferior and properly enslaved.

(2) The colonial impulse towards territorial expansion reflected the economic interests of slave owners as well as European immigrants' desire for economic independence. It was possible to gain territory only by taking it from indigenous nations. Europeans assumed that their claims outweighed indigenous rights, and this was reinforced by the European notion that Native Americans were culturally inferior savages.

These two aspects of the color line can be seen at work in nineteenth century American history. Until the Civil War, the most affluent and influential Americans (mainly owners of Southern plantations with many slaves) sought the unlimited expansion of slavery. That was resisted by many white Americans who sought economic independence by moving west, but who also wished to exclude people of color – be they black, red, yellow, or brown. The federal government then engaged in all-out war against the Plains Indians in order to acquire most of their territories. At the same time, the government was unwilling to enforce the legal rights of African Americans. Politically influential white Americans of North and South saw their interests as converging in the development of Jim Crow, which was accompanied by intense color line violence and propaganda.

(3) The attitudinal aspect of the color line takes many forms and functions somewhat independently of economic interests. Horrific cruelty over and above blatant murder was exhibited, for example, in slave-management practices and later in public lynchings. These actions (in which citizens of high as well as low social status participated) manifest extreme forms of racial hatred. At the other end of the attitudinal spectrum, we find whites who are repelled by such conduct but accept racial subordination, which they help enforce, or who are minimally troubled by racist practices and their legacy.

(4) History shows that current racial stratification results largely from public policies that are rationalized, reinforced, and maintained by white supremacist ideology. The color line persists, despite campaigns for reform, because it is deeply entrenched in the economy and in attitudes among whites that range from racial hatred to moral indifference. To weaken the color line, we must address the ideology of white supremacy as well as material inequities.

(5) Nineteenth and twentieth century history shows that reform is possible, but only by persistent effort; that we cannot predict which reform campaigns will be effective; that resistance to moderate reform is often violent; and that backlash can undo reforms. Consider some twentieth century examples.

Three young Japanese Americans challenged internment-related orders during World War II. They were unsuccessful and paid the price, but decades later a campaign to vindicate their resistance to racial injustice led to the federal government's acknowledging the wrongness of internment and providing reparations for its survivors. It is important that the corrective measures taken went beyond an apology – although the reparations paid did not nearly compensate even for the material losses of internees.

The African American students of Moton High School in Prince Edward County, Virginia, went on strike to demand equal schooling. Their efforts merged with similar actions by others, at a propitious time, and led to the Supreme Court's ruling in *Brown v. Board of Education*. That groundbreaking decision was followed by rulings against state-mandated segregation in other contexts, such as municipal transportation. Despite the end of *de jure* segregation, however, public schools across America remain segregated.

Four black college students in Greensboro, North Carolina, sought service at a whites-only lunch counter. Their persistent efforts sparked a regional campaign that desegregated many retail stores in the Jim Crow South and led to the founding of the Student Nonviolent Coordinating Committee, which conducted the most difficult and dangerous civil rights campaigns in the Jim Crow South.

An effort by four major civil rights organizations to enroll black voters in Mississippi was met with lethal violence, and few African Americans managed to register. What provoked national concern was the fact that two of the murdered voting rights activists were white. A group of Native Americans seized Alcatraz Island, the site of a closed federal prison. They claimed it, under treaty provisions, as surplus federal land, and scores held it for more than a year. They did not succeed in establishing a cultural center on the site, as they had hoped to do, but their action inspired many reform campaigns and helped to end the federal government's policy of "terminating" tribes, thereby protecting federal treaty obligations to provide desperately needed support. Congress passed the Voting Rights Act not long after Bloody Sunday, when peaceful marchers were violently assaulted by police in Selma, Alabama. Enforcement of the Act enabled many black Southerners to register and vote, some of whom were elected to public office. Recently, however, the Supreme Court has nullified important provisions of the Act, thereby allowing states to erect new "color-blind" barriers to voting that disproportionately disfranchise Americans of color.

(6) The history of grassroots action includes innumerable other campaigns for reform. Some have succeeded in weakening the color line, some have failed. Without such actions, however, there would be no progress at all. Even small steps improve lives, ease debilitating stress, promote human dignity, nurture mutual respect – and sometimes lead to larger reforms.

(7) Some reforms directly attack racial bias, while "color-blind" reforms aid people of color disproportionately. Some reforms can be achieved by relatively simple measures, like a regulation change, while others require the overhaul of major systems. Let us consider some examples.

Some improvements have been achieved in the criminal law. Reform campaigns have led, for example, to the tempering of biased sentencing laws (such as vastly more severe punishments for the possession of crack cocaine than for possession of powder cocaine). But the War on Drugs has led to mass incarceration, with enormous human cost.

The fiscal cost of imprisoning millions has led some states to begin reducing their prison populations. Shrinkage could be accelerated by ending the imprisonment of nonviolent offenders and elderly inmates. Reducing recidivism by improving post-release conditions requires, for example, much better access to housing (which requires, in turn, changes in public housing regulations); much better access to jobs (which requires rehabilitative prison programs); and much better access to normal civilian life (which should include restoring the franchise to past offenders). The reversal of wrongful convictions is being pursued by privately sponsored groups, such as the Innocence Project, which merit full public sector cooperation and support.

The continued hold of the color line on official activity is manifested in persistent racial profiling and police killings of unarmed people of color. Very recently, however, grassroots reactions to public and private anti-black violence and the like have led to the development of the "Black Lives Matter" movement.

Other examples reveal the limits of piecemeal reform. Fully funding and widening eligibility for food stamps, for instance, could greatly reduce food insecurity, which disproportionately affects people of color. Nutritional needs would be more fully met, however, by ensuring adequate household incomes, e.g., by creating jobs, substantially raising wage rates, and providing adequate incomes for those unable to work. Such measures would involve enormous changes in public policy, about which more presently.

Fully funding, widening the eligibility for, and increasing the value of Section 8 rental vouchers could greatly aid families in need of housing, who disproportionately include people of color. Housing needs would be more fully met, however, by substantially increasing the stock of affordable housing. But that too would require major changes in public policy.

As the two federal programs just mentioned already exist, their expansion could readily be provided by Congress. But Congress has been unwilling to fully fund either program, even within its current narrow constraints. And neither program addresses the underlying needs.

Recent grassroots campaigns for higher minimum wage rates at state and municipal levels have had modest favorable impact, and every dollar makes a difference to low income households. But too many households lack a livable income, even with one or two full-time workers. How can that deficit be addressed? How can we equalize life prospects for white and non-white infants? In turning to those questions, we must consider once again two issues that are central to the color line in America: segregation in housing and schools, and the wealth gap between white and non-white households. Residential segregation helps to ensure the continuation of school segregation and contributes appreciably to the wealth gap between white and non-white households and to the corresponding gap in life prospects.

Consider the wealth gap. To rectify the arrangements that have prevented people of color from acquiring assets, such as private homes, the system must significantly subsidize home acquisition by members of the populations that were targeted by policies such as red-lining. To equalize life prospects more generally, the system must make substantial investments – in affordable housing and public services, such as public transportation, safe child care, schools that nurture all children, and readily accessible medical care. As the entrenched racial inequities result largely from public policies, the cost of such programs could reasonably be paid by taxing the resources of those who have profited from the color-coded caste system.

None of this can be accomplished and maintained without attacking the attitudinal component of the color line. This will require government at all levels to engage in a carefully developed long-term program of fully explaining how wrongful policies supported the color line and created the need for corrective action. A government so committed would also reject racial profiling, unwarranted assaults on people of color, and the like.

Two special points must be added. First, US policies in Central America have undermined or overthrown democratically elected governments and supported dictators who are friendly to American corporations. As these policies have contributed substantially to the crises that now drive many asylum-seekers to America's borders, the US has a special obligation (beyond general considerations of humanity) to welcome them and facilitate their inclusion in American society.

Second, Native American communities have been disastrously affected by the expansionist policies that led to massive losses of life and the expropriation of almost all Native American land. These losses have been exacerbated by America's failure to respect its treaty commitments, to respect American Indian culture and sacred sites, and to secure contractual royalties for natural resources extracted from Indian land. Justice requires a reversal of those policies and a return of significant territory. America would do well by beginning with a return of the sacred land that includes Mount Rushmore, which constitutes an insult in stone.

These sketchy ideas suggest how the color line can be attacked. Each of the issues mentioned merits a campaign for reform, many of the issues are being addressed by committed advocates for a more equitable America, and their collective experience reveals the magnitude of the changes that are required for elimination of the color line.

BIBLIOGRAPHY

Acuña, Rodolfo. *Occupied America: A History of Chicanos.* Longman, 2000.

Alexander, Michelle. *The New Jim Crow: Mass Incarceration in the Age of Colorblindness.* New Press, 2010.

Allen, Theodore. *The Invention of the White Race.* Verso, 1994.

Aptheker, Herbert, ed. *A Documentary History of the Negro People in the United States.* 7 vols. Citadel, 1969.

Balderrama, Francisco, and E. Raymond Rodriguez. *Decade of Betrayal: Mexican Repatriation in the 1930s.* University of New Mexico Press, 2006 (rev.).

Berlin, Ira. *Many Thousands Gone: The First Two Centuries of Slavery in America.* Harvard University Press, 1998.

_____. *The Making of African America: The Four Great Migrations.* Viking, 2010.

_____. *The Long Emancipation: The Demise of Slavery in the United States.* Harvard University Press, 2015.

Blackmon, Douglas A. *Slavery by Another Name: The Re-enslavement of Black People in America from the Civil War to World War II.* Doubleday, 2008.

Blight, David W. *Frederick Douglass: Prophet of Freedom.* Simon & Schuster, 2018.

Branch, Taylor. *Parting the Waters: America in the King Years, 1954–63.* Simon & Schuster, 1968.

_____. *Pillar of Fire: America in the King Years, 1963–65.* Simon & Schuster, 1998.

Breitman, George, ed. *Malcolm X Speaks: Selected Speeches and Statements.* Grove Press, 1965.

Brodkin, Karen. *How Jews Became White Folks and What That Says About Race in America.* Rutgers University Press, 2000.

Bulmer-Thomas, Victor. *Empire in Retreat: The Past, Present, and Future of the United States.* Yale University Press, 2018.

Butler, Jon, ed. *Oxford Research Encyclopedia of American History.* Oxford University Press, 2016. Oxfordre.com/americanhistory

Carson, Clayborne, et al., eds. *The Eyes on the Prize Civil Rights Reader: Documents, Speeches, and Firsthand Accounts from the Black Freedom Struggle, 1954–1990.* Penguin Books, 1991.

Coffman, Tom. *Nation Within: The History of the American Occupation of Hawai'i.* Duke University Press, 2016.

Corlett, J. Angelo. *Race, Racism, and Reparations.* Cornell University Press, 2003.

Crawford, V.L., J.A. Rouse, and B. Woods, eds. *Women in the Civil Rights Movement: Trailblazers and Torchbearers, 1941–1965.* Indiana University Press, 1993.

Daniels, Roger. *Asian America: Chinese and Japanese in the United States Since 1850.* University of Washington Press, 1988.

Davis, David Brion. *The Problem of Slavery in Western Culture.* Cornell University Press, 1966.

_____. *Inhuman Bondage: The Rise and Fall of Slavery in the New World.* Oxford University Press, 2006.

Delbanco, Andrew. *The War Before the War: Fugitive Slaves and the Struggle for America's Soul from the Revolution to the Civil War.* Penguin, 2018.

Deloria, Vine, Jr., and Clifford M. Lytle. *American Indians, American Justice.* University of Texas Press, 1983.

Douglass, Frederick. "The Color Line," *North American Review*, vol. 132, 1881.

_____. *Narrative of the Life of Frederick Douglass, an American Slave.* Oxford University Press, 1999.

Du Bois, W.E.B. *Black Reconstruction in America: An Essay Toward a History of the Part Which Black Folk Played in the Attempt to Reconstruct Democracy in America, 1860–1880.* In *The Oxford W.E.B. Du Bois*, vol. 6. Oxford University Press, 2007.

_____. *The Souls of Black Folk.* Oxford University Press, 2007.

Feagin, Joe R. *Racist America: Roots, Current Realities, and Future Reparations.* Routledge, 2000.

_____. *Systemic Racism: A Theory of Oppression.* Routledge, 2006.

Foner, Eric. *Reconstruction: America's Unfinished Revolution, 1863–1877.* Harper & Row, 1988.

_____. *The Second Founding: How the Civil War and Reconstruction Remade the Constitution.* Norton, 2019.

Forman, James, Jr. *Locking up Our Own: Crime and Punishment in Black America.* Farrar, Straus & Giroux, 2017.

Gallagher, Gary W., and Alan T. Nolan, eds. *The Myth of the Lost Cause and Civil War History.* Indiana University Press, 2000.

Genovese, Eugene D. *Roll, Jordan, Roll: The World the Slaves Made.* Vintage, 1974.

Gibson, Carrie. *El Norte: The Epic and Forgotten Story of Hispanic North America.* Grove/Atlantic, 2019.

Gilens, Martin. *Why Americans Hate Welfare: Race, Media, and the Politics of Antipoverty Policy.* University of Chicago Press, 1999.

Grenier, John. *The First Way of War: American War Making on the Frontier, 1607–1814.* Cambridge University Press, 2005.

Hening, W.W., ed. *The Statutes at Large, Being a Collection of All the Laws of Virginia, from the First Session of the Legislature, in 1619.* Samuel Pleasants, 1809–23.

Hill, Lance. *The Deacons for Defense: Armed Resistance and the Civil Rights Movement.* University of North Carolina Press, 2004.

Hinton, Elizabeth Kai. *From the War on Poverty to the War on Crime: The Making of Mass Incarceration in America.* Harvard University Press, 2016.

Holton, Woody. *Unruly Americans and the Origins of the Constitution.* Hill & Wang, 2007.

Ignatiev, Noel. *How the Irish Became White.* Routledge, 1994.

Immerwahr, Daniel. *How to Hide an Empire: A History of the Greater United States.* Farrar, Straus & Giroux, 2019.

Irons, Peter H. *Justice at War: The Story of the Japanese-American Internment Cases.* University of California Press, 1993.

Jacobson, Matthew Frye. *Whiteness of a Different Color: European Immigrants and the Alchemy of Race.* Harvard University Press, 1999.

Jennings, Francis. *The Invasion of America: Indians, Colonialism, and the Cant of Conquest.* Norton, 1975.

Kolchin, Peter. *American Slavery, 1619–1877.* Hill and Wang, 1993.

Lichtman, Allan J. *The Embattled Vote in America: From the Founding to the Present.* Harvard University Press. 2018.

Litwack, Leon F. *North of Slavery: The Negro in the Free States, 1790–1860.* University of Chicago Press, 1961.

Loury, Glenn C. *The Anatomy of Racial Inequality.* Harvard University Press, 2002.

Lyons, David. *Confronting Injustice: Moral History and Political Theory.* Oxford University Press, 2013.

Madley, Benjamin. *An American Genocide: The United States and the California Indian Catastrophe, 1846–1873.* Yale University Press, 2016.

Malcolm X. *By Any Means Necessary.* Pathfinder, 1992.

Marable, Manning. *Race, Reform, and Rebellion: The Second Reconstruction and Beyond in Black America, 1945–2006.* University Press of Mississippi, 2007.

_____. *Malcolm X: A Life of Reinvention.* Viking, 2011.

Massey, Douglas S., and Nancy A. Denton. *American Apartheid: Segregation and the Making of the Underclass.* Harvard University Press, 1993.

Merritt, Keri Leigh. *Masterless Men: Poor Whites and Slavery in the Antebellum South.* Cambridge University Press, 2017.

Morgan, Edmund S. *American Slavery, American Freedom: The Ordeal of Colonial Virginia..* Norton, 1975.

Morris, Thomas. *Southern Slavery and the Law, 1619–1860.* University of North Carolina Press, 1996.

Myrdal, Gunnar, et al. *An American Dilemma: The Negro Problem and American Democracy.* McGraw-Hill, 1944.

Nash, Gary. *Red, White, and Black: The Peoples of Early North America.* Pearson/Prentice Hall, 2006.

National Advisory Commission on Civil Disorders. *The Kerner Report.* Princeton University Press, 2016.

Ngai, Mae. *Impossible Subjects: Illegal Aliens and the Making of Modern America.* Princeton University Press, 2004.

Okrent, Daniel. *The Guarded Gate: Bigotry, Eugenics, and the Law That Kept Two Generations of Jews, Italians, and Other European Immigrants out of America.* Scribner, 2019.

Oliver, Melvin L, and Thomas M. Shapiro. *Black Wealth / White Wealth: A New Perspective on Racial Inequality.* Routledge, 2006.

Orfield, G., and C. Ashkinaze. *The Closing Door: Conservative Policy and Black Opportunity.* University of Chicago Press, 1991.

_____, G., and S. Eaton. *Dismantling Desegregation: The Quiet Reversal of Brown v. Board of Education.* New Press, 1996.

Painter, Nell Irvin. *The History of White People.* Norton, 2010.

Peck, James. *Freedom Ride.* Simon and Schuster, 1962.

President's Committee on Civil Rights. *To Secure These Rights: Report of the President's Committee on Civil Rights.* U.S. Government Printing Office, 1947.

Roediger, David. *Working Toward Whiteness: How America's Immigrants Became White – The Strange Journey from Ellis Island to the Suburbs.* Basic Books, 2005.

Rose, Willie Lee, ed. *A Documentary History of Slavery in North America*. University of Georgia Press, 1999.

Rothstein, Richard. *The Color of Law: A Forgotten History of How Our Government Segregated America*. Liveright Publishing Corporation, 2017.

Schirmer, D.B., and S.R. Shalom, eds. *The Philippines Reader: A History of Colonialism, Neocolonialism, Dictatorship, and Resistance*. South End Press, 1987.

Shelby, Tommie. *Dark Ghettos: Injustice, Dissent, and Reform*. Harvard University Press, 2016.

———, and Brandon M. Terry, eds. *To Shape a New World: Essays on the Political Philosophy of Martin Luther King, Jr.* Harvard University Press, 2018.

Shellow, Robert, ed. *The Harvest of American Racism: The Political Meaning of Violence in the Summer of 1967*. University of Michigan Press. 2018.

Silva, Noenoe K. *Aloha Betrayed: Native Hawaiian Resistance to American Colonialism*. Duke University Press, 2004.

Stuckey, Sterling. *Slave Culture: Nationalist Theory and the Foundations of Black America*. Oxford University Press, 2014.

Takaki, Ronald. *Strangers from a Different Shore: A History of Asian Americans*. Little, Brown, 1998.

———. *A Different Mirror: A History of Multicultural America*. Little, Brown, 2008.

Terrill, Robert, ed. *The Cambridge Companion to Malcolm X*. Cambridge University Press, 2010.

Thoreau, Henry David. *Reform Papers*, ed. W. Glick. Princeton University Press, 1973.

Treuer, David. *The Heartbeat of Wounded Knee: Native America from 1890 to the Present*. Penguin, 2019.

United States Commission on Civil Rights. *Broken Promises: Continuing Federal Funding Shortfall for Native Americans*. US Government Printing Office, 2018.

Urofsky, M.I., and P. Finkelman, eds. *Documents of American Constitutional and Legal History*. Oxford University Press, 2008.

Waldrep, Christopher, ed. *Lynching in America: A History in Documents*. New York University Press, 2006.

Wallace, Anthony F.C. *The Long, Bitter Trail: Andrew Jackson and the Indians*. Hill and Wang, 1997.

Washburn, Wilcomb E. *Red Man's Land/White Man's Law: The Past and Present Status of the American Indian*. University of Oklahoma Press, 1995.

Washington, James Melvin, ed. *A Testament of Hope: The Essential Writings of Martin Luther King, Jr.* HarperOne, 1991.

Wells, Ida B. *Southern Horrors and Other Writings: The Anti-lynching Campaign of Ida B. Wells, 1892–1900*. Bedford Books, 2016.

Wilkerson, Isabel. *The Warmth of Other Suns: The Epic Story of America's Great Migration*. Random House, 2010.

Williams, Robert F. *Negroes with Guns*. Marzani & Munsell, 1962.

Wilson, William Julius. *More Than Just Race: Being Black and Poor in the Inner City*. Norton, 2009.

Woodward, C. Vann. *The Strange Career of Jim Crow*. Oxford University Press, 2002.

Wright, Richard. *Uncle Tom's Children*. Harper & Row, 1940.

Zinn, Howard. *A People's History of the United States 1492-Present*. Harper/Collins, 2003.

INDEX

Made in the USA
Las Vegas, NV
29 January 2022

42582226R00085